HOW MANY?

Charles Snape and Heather Scott

CLHBEC

CAMBRIDGE UNIVERSITY PRESS

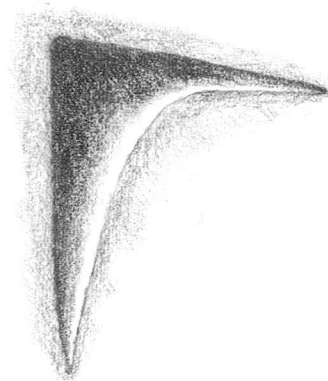

Published by the Press Syndicate of the University of Cambridge
The Pitt Building, Trumpington Street, Cambridge CB2 1RP
40 West 20th Street, New York, NY 10011-4211, USA
10 Stamford Road, Oakleigh, Melbourne 3166, Australia

© Cambridge University Press 1995

First published 1995

Printed in Great Britain at the University Press, Cambridge.

ISBN 0 521 45953 2 Paperback.

Library of Congress cataloguing in publication data

Snape, Charles.
How many / Charles Snape and Heather Scott
   p.   cm.
ISBN 0 521 45953 2 (pbk)
1. Mathematics – Juvenile literature. [1. Mathematics.]
I. Scott, Heather. II. Title.
QA40.5.S57 1994
513 – dc20 94-15301 CIP

Design, illustration and artwork by
Juliet and Charles Snape Limited

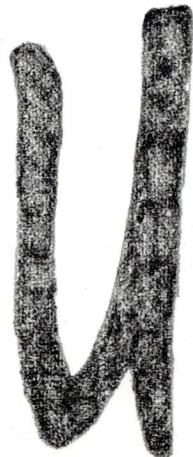

Contents

One, two and many

This shepherd of ancient times lets her goats out in the morning to graze on the surrounding hills. At night she brings them back to the compound. How can she be sure that she has brought back the same number that she let out?

When people first lived on this planet they probably did not need to count. People lived in small groups and having little or no trade within their community simply had no need of a number more than two. Even quite recently, communities which have had little contact with the outside world, have been discovered and to them everything that was more than two was 'many'.

How and why did counting start?

At some time in the distant past people settled down and began to grow crops and domesticate animals. Sometimes there were surplus stocks, and so trading began. There was therefore a need to keep some kind of accounts. This meant that some way of counting had to be invented. Did the shepherd look at her hands and think 'ah, each finger can stand for one goat'? Maybe when she got to ten – two hands – she started to use her toes, or perhaps she thought 'I could put a stone in a bag to represent each ten.' *Can you see how she might start doing simple addition and subtraction?*

It may have been her daughter or her granddaughter who came up with the big breakthrough that you could have fours or fives of different things – four goats, four apples, four trees. This is known as the fourness or fiveness. It may have been at this stage that numbers began to get names. *How would you go about giving numbers names?* In one Asian language the word for five is the same as the word for hand.

To all these generations of shepherds ten would have seemed a natural break: you could have four tens plus a hand of goats or three tens and two thumbs of bags of wheat. So how would you describe eleven? The word comes from an earlier word which means one more than ten;

similarly, twelve means two more than ten. *What would you say for three more than ten or four more than ten ...? Do you think that when you got to ten tens you might need a new name? When would you need a new number name after that?*

Names for numbers

Below are some possible names for numbers. Can you think which they stand for? Can you think of number names up to ten? A new name for one hundred?

Finger	Eyes	Feyes	Limbs

Why 10?

Probably because of the number of fingers we have, our number system is based on 10. 10 seems the natural base to use – but not quite as natural as you might think. How many seconds in a minute? Minutes in an hour? Degrees in a circle? To Ancient Babylonian priests the natural base was 60. Other civilisations developed number systems using different bases.

How many?

Look at each of the pictures below, one at a time, for about a second. Make a guess at the number of bison in each picture without counting. *When do you start to guess wrongly?*

Pounds, shillings and pence

Until 1971, people in Britain used a money system which had three different bases. When the system was changed there was quite an outcry with people complaining that the decimals were too difficult! Pence (d) are in base 12, shillings (s) are in base 20 and pounds (£) are in base 10. *Can you do the following sums? Which system do you think is best?*

```
  £    s    d          £    s    d
 10    5   11         19    7    9
+ 3   19    7        - 8    9    6
 ■    ■    ■          ■    ■    ■

  £    s    d          £    s    d
  9   19    9         ■    ■    ■
×          3        3│10    8    6
 ■    ■    ■
```

5

Hindu number system

A million, a billion, a trillion,... we take numbers very much for granted these days. But it has not always been so.

We take it for granted that we can count beyond a million and have ways of expressing any number we choose. Yet this ability eluded scholars for thousands of years.

The key is in the use of the symbol for zero, 0, invented by the Hindus in India, probably sometime between AD 400 and 800.

The development of our modern numerals began in the Indus Valley. Evidence for this can be found carved on pillars over 2200 years old. By AD 850 all nine digits were being represented by different symbols, which weren't based on letters of an alphabet or pictograms. As the digits developed so did zero. At first it was a dot, to represent an empty column on an abacus. It was from the abacus that the Hindus also developed place value. Imaginary columns based on powers of ten represent the real columns of the abacus. Using place value, any of the digits can stand for something different. 5 can be used in 5 for five units, 50 for fifty (five tens), 500 (five hundred) and so on.

With these three developments – the nine digits, a symbol for zero and place value – came the ability to do calculations entirely with symbols, without needing an abacus.

Place value
The collection of digits above is quite meaningless, but by organising them into columns they can take on a number of meanings.

Thousands	Hundreds	Tens	Units
4	5	0	7
7	0	5	4

How many different 4-figure numbers can you make by re-arranging the digits 4507?

Powers of ten
Our number system (decimal) is based on powers of ten. When we have collected a group of ten we need to indicate this by using new columns:

Millions	Hundreds of Thousands	Tens of Thousands	Thousands	Hundreds	Tens	Units
10^6	10^5	10^4	10^3	10^2	10^1	10^0
10 × 10 × 10 × 10 × 10 × 10 × 10	10 × 10 × 10 × 10 × 10 × 10	10 × 10 × 10 × 10	10 × 10 × 10	10 × 10	10	1

This system can be developed indefinitely.

Our numerals are often called Arabic, because they came to Western Europe via the Arab civilisation. Originally the Arabs wrote out numbers word by word, even when calculating complex sums. Some mathematicians used the Ancient Greek method of representing numbers with letters but a breakthrough was made when they discovered the Indian numerals and the Hindu decimal system.

An Arab mathematician called Musa al-Khwarizmi studied the Hindu system and in AD 825 explained it in a book which, roughly translated, is called 'A Book about addition and subtraction according to the Hindu method of calculation'. However, this Arabic knowledge was not to reach Western Europe for another 300 years.

Zero sums
Is it possible to do all these sums?

100 + 0 = ■	100 ÷ 0 = ■	0 × 100 = ■
0 − 100 = ■	0 + 100 = ■	0 ÷ 100 = ■
100 × 0 = ■	100 − 0 = ■	

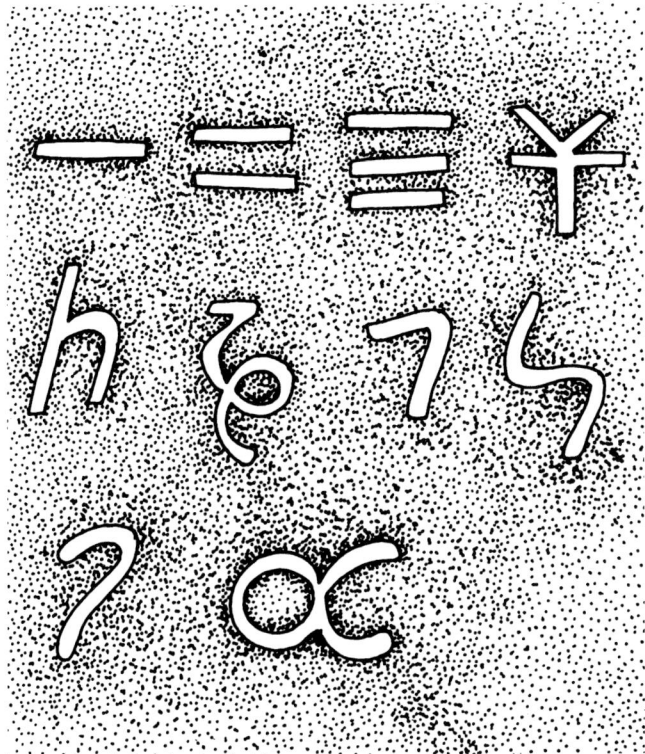

The early form of Indian numerals found in a cave in Nasik, near Bombay, India. They are at least 1800 years old. By AD 1300 these had developed in Europe into the shapes below.

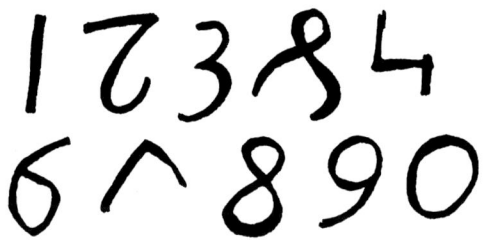

Liber abaci

The person credited with introducing the use of Hindu numerals into Western Europe was an Italian called Fibonacci, who lived from 1170 to 1250. In his youth he had travelled widely, visiting Africa, the Middle East and possibly India. In later years, Fibonacci became famous as a mathematician and took part in many mathematical contests that were being held at that time.

In 1202 Fibonacci published a book called *Liber abaci*. The start of *Liber abaci* demonstrates how 'with the nine Indian figures and the Arab sign 0 any number can be written'. He went on to explain how these numerals could be used to do arithmetic.

> I'm a 2-digit Fibonacci number and I am prime. The square of my number is a 3-digit number.

On the cards

Fibonacci introduced into Western Europe a number series that were to bear his name These are the first few Fibonacci numbers. *Can you work out out how they are generated?*

1, 1, 2, 3, 5, 8, 13, ...

The number card has its back to us. It is describing the number on its front. *Can you work out what it is?* Make up some puzzles of your own.

Number series

These number series were published in 1713 in a book called *Artis Conjectandi* by Jacob Bernoulli.

Can you work out the rules for making them?

1	1	1	1	1	1	1	1	1	1	1	1
1	2	3	4	5	6	7	8	9	10	11	12
1	3	6	10	15	21	28	36	45	55	66	78
1	4	1	20	35	56	84	120	165	220	286	364
1	5	0	35	70	126	210	330	495	715	1001	1365
1	6	1	56	126	252	462	792	1287	2002	3003	4368
1	7	5	84	210	462	924	1716	3003	5005	8008	12376
1	8	2	120	330	792	1716	3432	6435	11440	19448	31824
1	9	1	16	49	1287	3003	6435	12870	24310	43758	75582
1	1	2	5	5	2002	5005	11440	24310	48620	92378	16796

Pythagorean triples and triangles

The Ancient Egyptians used a rope with 13 equally spaced knots in it to mark out square corners of fields when they measured out their land. This was done regularly as the farmers were taxed on the size of their fertile fields along the banks of the Nile which were often flooded, and bits of them would be swept away. A similar system was used in China for land surveying.

The (3, 4, 5) triangle is a right-angled triangle. If you square each of the numbers you will find that the two smaller square numbers add together to make the larger square number:

3   4   5
9   16   25
9 + 16 = 25

Groups of three numbers with this property are called *Pythagorean triples*, after the Greek mathematician Pythagoras, who lived in the 6th century BC.

The Hindus in India also needed to use right angles. In addition to the (3, 4, 5) triangle which the Egyptians discovered they found that the following right-angled triangles had the same property:

(12, 16, 20)   (8, 15, 17)   (12, 35, 37)
(15, 20, 25)   (5, 12, 13)   (15, 36, 39)

Some of these can be made by using the (3, 4, 5) triangle and multiplying each number in the triple by another number. For example:

$$3 \quad 4 \quad 5$$
$$\times 4 \quad \times 4 \quad \times 4$$
$$= 12 \quad 16 \quad 20$$

Some of the triples are *primitive triples*, for example (3, 4, 5), because the numbers cannot be found from another set of triples by multiplying. *Which of the Hindu triples are primitive? Which have been made by multiplying a primitive triple by a common multiplier?*

Here are the first 12 primitive triples: (3, 4, 5) (5, 12, 13) (8, 15, 17) (7, 24, 25) (20, 21, 29) (12, 35, 37) (9, 40, 41) (28, 45, 53) (11, 60, 61) (16, 63, 65) (33, 56, 65) (48, 55, 73). There are 158 primitive triples where the three numbers add up to less than 1000. *How many can you find?*

Diophantus and the early Greeks used formulas to generate Pythagorean triples. Choose two numbers m and n and put the numbers into each of the following formulas:

To find the first answer do $m^2 - n^2$
To find the second answer do $2mn$
To find the third answer do $m^2 + n^2$

By using these formulas it is possible to find some interesting patterns in Pythagorean triples.

● Use pairs of consecutive numbers for m and n to generate Pythagorean triples – *what do all the triples have in common?*

● Use pairs of triangle numbers for m and n to generate Pythagorean triples – *what do all the triples have in common?*

Making Pythagorean puzzles

Square to square

Draw 2 squares accurately next to each other. Label each of the corners of the squares.

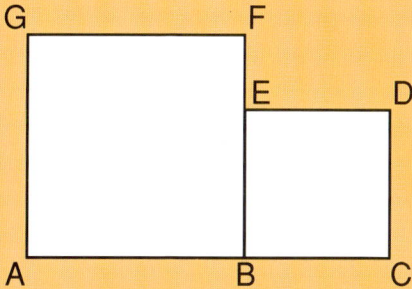

Put another point (H) on the diagram so that the distance from A to H is exactly the same length as the side of the smaller square (B to C).

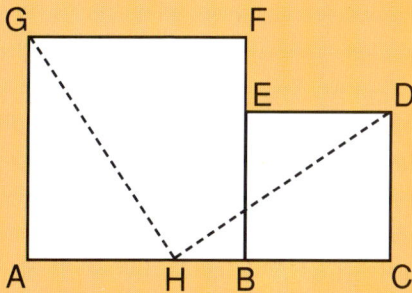

Now draw a line from G to H and from H to D.

Cut out each of the five pieces you now have and put them together to make one larger square.

Perigal's dissection

A mathematician, Perigal, showed in 1873 that it is possible to use three cuts to divide two squares into five pieces which can always be re-formed into one square.

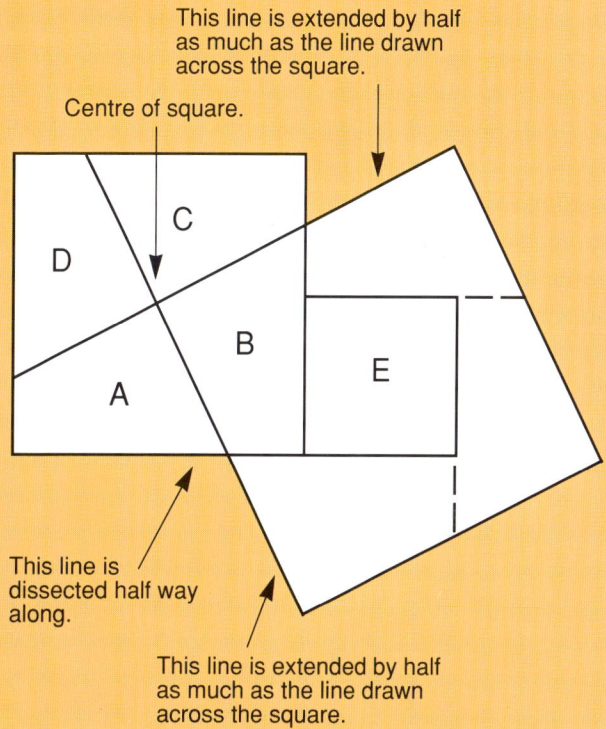

This line is extended by half as much as the line drawn across the square.

Centre of square.

This line is dissected half way along.

This line is extended by half as much as the line drawn across the square.

Cut pieces A, C, D and slide them into place on the larger square.

Triangles to spirals

In the centre of a page draw a right-angled triangle with two sides exactly one unit long (say 1.5cm).

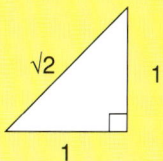

Draw a new right-angled triangle on the hypotenuse of the first triangle keeping the outside side one unit long – 1.5cm.

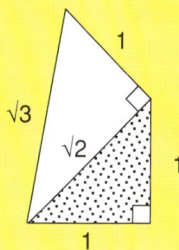

Continue this process. *What shape will you create?*

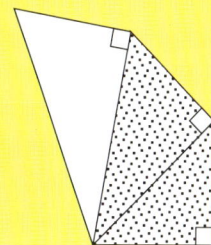

9

Numbers for Greeks

It is often thought that the study of mathematics originated in Ancient Greece. But, like all civilisations, the Greeks borrowed and learnt from other civilisations. What the Greeks gave us was the idea that mathematics could be studied for its own sake.

Unity

The number one was called *unity* by the Greeks. It was probably the Greeks who first divided numbers into odd and even. The Greek mathematicians, especially those who were followers of Pythagoras, began to look for meaning in numbers. It was the Greeks who first began the search for prime numbers. A prime number is a number that has only itself and unity as factors. A factor is a number that can be divided into another number with no remainder.

Perfect numbers

One type of number the Greeks found they called a *perfect number*. A perfect number is one where all its factors except itself sum to that number. The smallest perfect number is 6.

$$1 + 2 + 3 = 6$$

The next smallest is 28. Check it out!

The Greeks found only four perfect numbers between 1 and 10 000. *Can you find the other two?*

The perfect numbers 6 and 28 convinced the Pythagoreans that numbers in themselves had some secret meaning.

Imperfect numbers

An *imperfect number* is one where the sum of its factors is either lesser or greater than the number itself.

If the sum of the factors is less than the number itself then it is called *deficient*.

If the sum of the factors is more than the number then it is called *abundant*.

Can you classify these numbers into deficient and abundant imperfect numbers?

35, 42, 56, 64, 70, 84, 99, 102, 112, 155

Amicable numbers

Another group of numbers the Greeks discovered are called *amicable*. Amicable numbers are a pair of numbers whose factors sum to each other.

The smallest pair of amicable numbers is 220 and 284. If we add the factors of 220 we get:

$$1 + 2 + 4 + 5 + 10 + 11 + 20 + 22 + 44 + 55 + 110 = 284$$

and if we sum the factors of 284 we get:

$$1 + 2 + 4 + 71 + 142 = 220$$

1184 and 1210 are another pair of amicable numbers. Check them out.

The story of amicable numbers so far ...

All our knowledge of Greek mathematics comes to us very much second hand. There are no surviving manuscripts and the copies that exist are copies of copies. However, we are fairly certain that Pythagoras would have known the lowest pair of amicable numbers, but we have no way of knowing if he knew of any others.

For about 1200 years after the Greeks no one seems to have come up with any more until another pair were found in 1635 by the French mathematician Pierre de Fermat. His pair were 17 296 and 18 416. At about the same time, another French mathematician, René Descartes, discovered another pair, 9 363 584 and 9 437 056.

It was to be another 100 years before any more amicable numbers turned up. The Swiss mathematician Euler published a list of 60 amicable numbers; unfortunately two of these prove not to be so!

It wasn't until 1830 that another pair was found by a French mathematician called Legendre. 37 years later, the mathematical world was astonished when a 16-year old Italian boy discovered another pair. What was even more astonishing was that this pair was the second lowest and had been overlooked by Western mathematicians for over 300 years. (This was the amicable pair 1184 and 1210.)

More than 600 amicable pairs are known today, many of which contain over 30 digits.

The Ancient Greeks adopted two methods of recording numbers that made doing sums almost impossible.

Attica symbols

The first method of recording numbers used by the Greeks was Attica, named after the area around Athens. It was not too dissimilar to the Egyptian way of writing numbers at that time. Our knowledge of the Ancient Greek Attica numbers comes mainly from fragments of pottery found many years after the Ancient Greek civilisation ceased. Between about 500 BC and 100 BC, writing, especially on things like pots, could be written left to right, right to left or one line left to right and the next line right to left. Above on the right is a table of the Greek Attica numbers.

Ι	Γ	Δ	Ρ	Η	Ϝ	Χ
1	5	10	50	100	500	1000

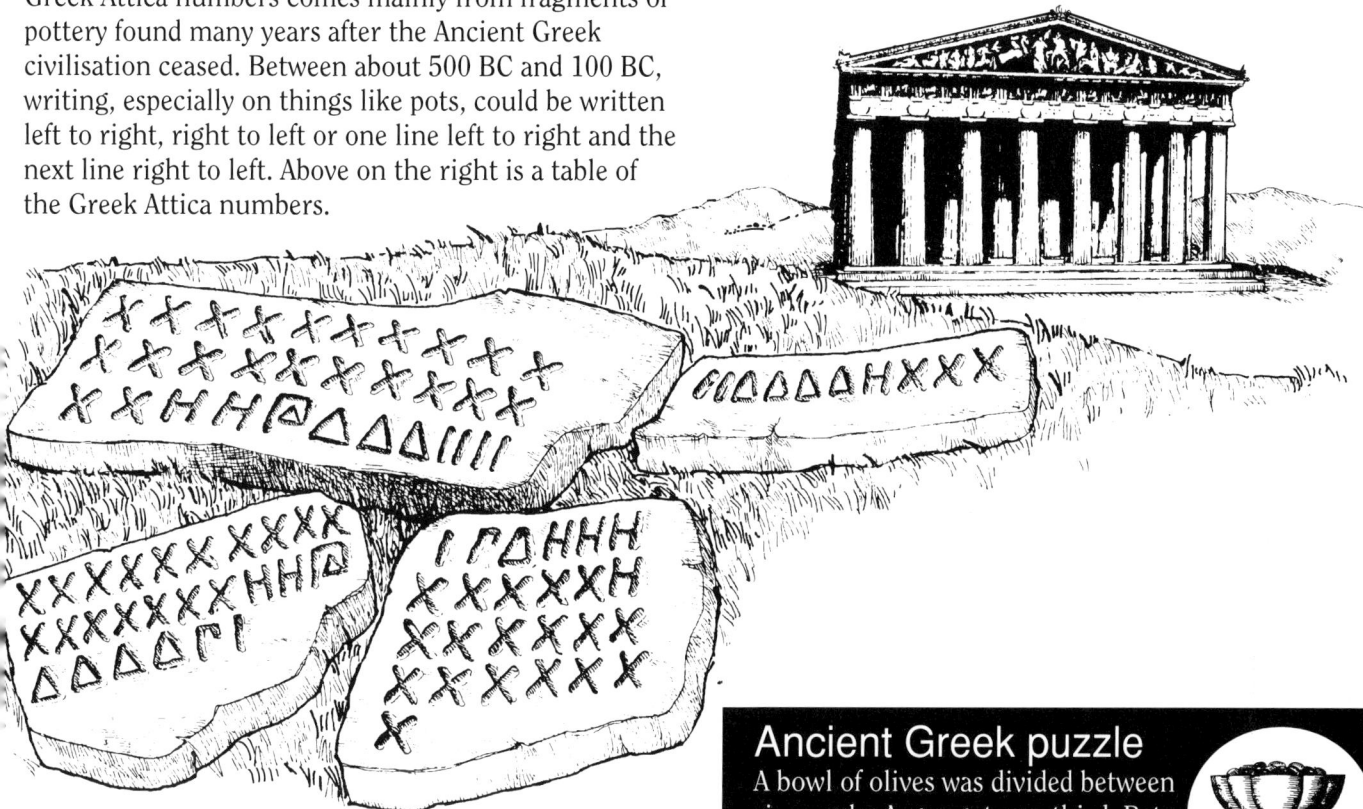

Can you work out what numbers are represented by these Attica symbol groupings shown on bits of broken pottery?

Ancient Greek puzzle

A bowl of olives was divided between six people. Argos got one-third, Beta got one-eighth, Cicely got a quarter and Delphi got a fifth. Elysium got ten olives and Furi got only one olive. *How many olives were there in the bowl originally?*

Ionic numbers

In the century before the birth of Christ, Attica had been replaced by another way of writing numbers, known as Ionic. The Greeks adopted a method developed by the Ancient Hebrews, which used letters of the alphabet to represent numbers. Not only did this make calculations with numbers very difficult, it also meant they had to invent new symbols because their alphabet contained only 24 letters. The Greeks worked in base 10.

Can you complete the 10 × 10 multiplication table opposite? The Greek letter Σ represented 200. Can you make a multiplication table up to 15 × 15?

	A	B	Γ	Δ	E	F	Z	H	Θ	I	
A	A	B	Γ	Δ	E	F	Z	H	Θ	I	A
B		Δ	F	H	I	IB				K	B
Γ										Λ	Γ
Δ										M	Δ
E					KE					N	E
F										Ξ	F
Z										O	Z
H									OB	Π	H
Θ										q	Θ
I										P	I

Really big numbers

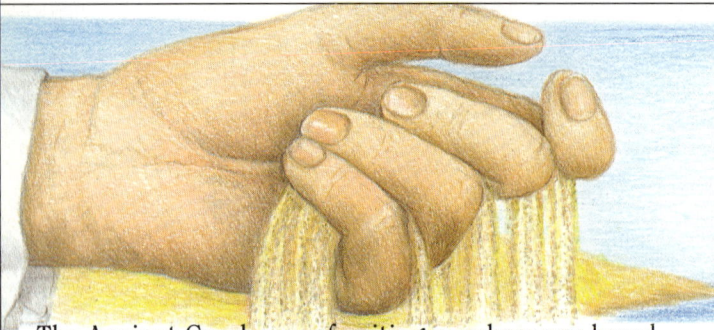

How many grains of sand are there in the world?

Too many to count ...?

The Ancient Greek way of writing numbers was based on letters of the alphabet. This made working with them very difficult and most arithmetic was carried out on an abacus. Working with letters also made the writing down of big numbers very clumsy. The Greeks had a word 'myriad' which meant 10 000, but to most people this was such a large number that they thought of it as meaning 'uncountable'.

'How many grains of sand are there in the world?' This was the question that the Greek mathematician, Archimedes (287–212 BC), posed in a book called *The Sand Reckoner*. 'How many grains of sand on a beach?' '...a million? ...a billion? ...a googol?' To most people at that time, the only way they could see to do this would be to sit on the beach and count each grain one at a time. This would take a very long time, and when they got past 10 000 they had no way of writing it down.

In his book, Archimedes described a way to count the sand by making bigger and bigger units. Start by counting how many grains of sand would equal a grain of wheat, then work out how much wheat would fit in a sack, how many sacks would fit in a boat, how many boats would fit on a beach and so on. The method he used to represent these bigger and bigger numbers was to have myriads of myriads (10 000 × 10 000) and myriads of that number and so on. In this way Archimedes was able to describe numbers that would have a one followed by millions of noughts.

How many grains?

Twenty grains of sand take up as much space as a grain of wheat. A beach is 500 metres long, 10 metres wide and 2 metres deep. *Can you work how many grains of sand the beach contains?* (You will first need to estimate how many grains of wheat there are in, say, 1 cubic cm.)

Powering up numbers

Another way of writing four is 2^2. This means 2×2. The small two means multiply the number by itself. $3^2 = 3 \times 3$, $4^2 = 4 \times 4$. The result of multiplying a number by itself is called a square number.

Another way of writing eight is 2^3. This means $2 \times 2 \times 2$. When a number is multiplied by itself in this way it is called a cube number.

Another way of writing sixteen is 2^4. This means $2 \times 2 \times 2 \times 2$. The small number is called an index. When a number is written with an index we say that the number is to the power of that index. For example:

4^5 is 4 to the power of 5, which is 1024.

Can you work these out?

$$5^4 \quad 6^2 \quad 7^3 \quad 4^6 \quad 2^{10}$$

Which of these pairs of numbers is the biggest?

7^7 or 90 000 5^5 or 3 000

900 000 or 4^9 18 or 9^2

800 or 8^3

Sky high numbers

Approximate distance in km from the Sun

Mercury	Venus	Jupiter	Saturn
58 000 000	110 000 000	770 000 000	1 427 000 000
Uranus	Neptune	Pluto	
2 800 000 000	4 400 000 000	5 900 000 000	

Altair (White star)	150 000 000 000 000
Sirius (White star)	82 000 000 000 000
Procyon (Yellow star)	104 000 000 000 000

Beta Centauri (Blue-white star, as bright as 10 000 Suns)
3 700 000 000 000 000

Above are some approximate distances from the Sun to some heavenly bodies. *Which is the third furthest from the Sun?* Astronomers and other scientists working with very large numbers need to have a less cumbersome way of writing them down. The method they use is called 'standard form'.

Standard form is based on powers of 10. So, for example, $10 \times 10 \times 10$ is written 10^3 (10 to the power of 3). $10 \times 10 \times 10 \times 10 \times 10$ would be written as 10^5. The distance from Mars to the Sun is approximately 200 000 000 km, which in standard form is 2×10^8. This is how it is worked out:

Really big number

Number between 1 and 10

$$200\,000\,000 = 2 \times 100\,000\,000$$
$$= 2 \times (10 \times 10 \times 10 \times 10 \times 10 \times 10 \times 10 \times 10)$$
$$= 2 \times 10^8$$

Power of 10

The distance Earth to the Sun is about 150 000 000 km, which in standard form is 1.5×10^8.

$$150\,000\,000 = 1.5 \times 100\,000\,000$$
$$= 1.5 \times (10 \times 10 \times 10 \times 10 \times 10 \times 10 \times 10 \times 10)$$
$$= 1.5 \times 10^8$$

Can you write the distances from the Sun to the heavenly bodies in standard form? Can you write the number of grains of sand on the beach in standard form?

Googol

For many centuries an old French word, million (probably from an older Italian word, *mille*, which meant 1000) proved adequate to describe the biggest numbers but with the increase in trade, the rise in money supply and inflation, new variants had to be coined. Thus we have billions, trillions and octillions. Each meant an almost uncountable number when first used. But what do you do when you want a name for an incredibly large number? The answer for one American mathematician was to go home and ask his young nephew, who came up with the word 'googol'. It had no particular meaning but the googol is now used in most languages to describe an incredibly large number – such as 1 followed by 100 noughts.

10^{100} = 100000000000000000000
00000000000000000000
00000000000000000000
00000000000000000000
00000000000000000000

Counting on

Abacus

Although no one knows who invented the abacus, or when, it is likely that it developed independently in different countries.

It is thought that the word abacus comes from a Hebrew word meaning dust. In Ancient Israel numbers were represented by the 20 letters of their alphabet plus an extra four characters. As with the Greek system, this made manipulating numbers – addition, subtraction, multiplication and division – almost impossible, so it was only used for official records of the government or religious authorities. Ordinary people used a much simpler method of covering a table with sand and using marks such as dots to do calculations. When a calculation was completed the sand would be brushed ready for a new one.

The Romans used a table with grooves carved on it. A Roman merchant would place small stones, called *calculi*, in the grooves. These stones would be moved up and down in the grooves to do calculations.

The form of abacus that we are most familiar with probably developed in China. The Chinese put balls on wires and hung them in a frame. As in the Roman system, the balls were moved up and down on the wires to do calculations. This is the system still in use in some parts of the world; various countries developed their own kind of abacus. Three are shown here.

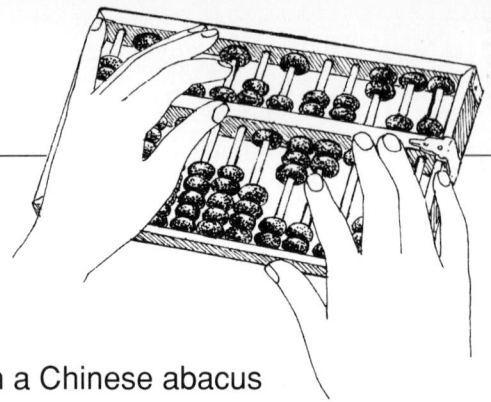

Numbers on a Chinese abacus

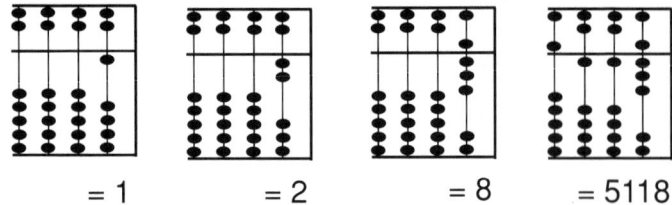

= 1   = 2   = 8   = 5118

Adding: 9 + 27

Put 9 on the abacus.

Add 20 by advancing 2 beads in the next column.

Add 1 by removing 4 and lowering 5.

Add 6 by advancing 10, removing 5, advancing 1.

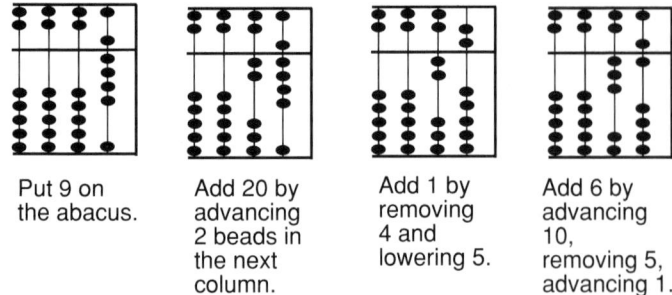

Read off the answer: 36

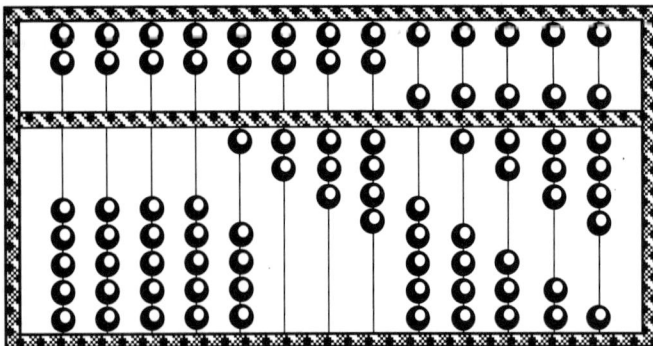

Above: Chinese abacus. Right: Russian abacus.
Below: Japanese abacus. One abacus shows 7483621954, the others show 7946.8723457694 and 123456789. *Can you work out which abacus shows which number?*

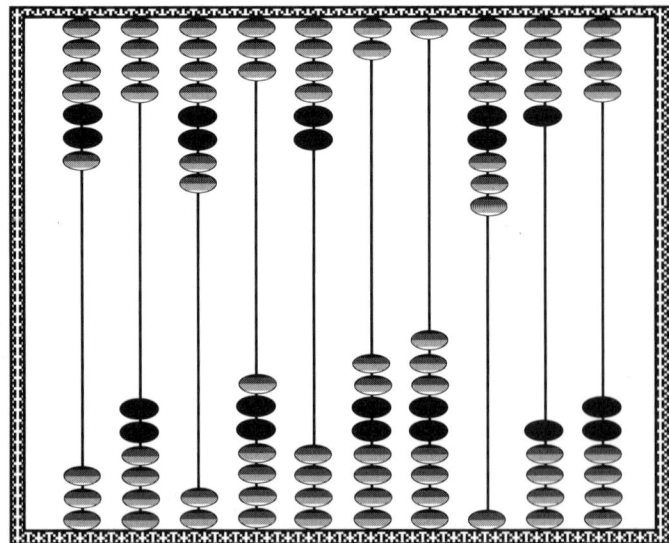

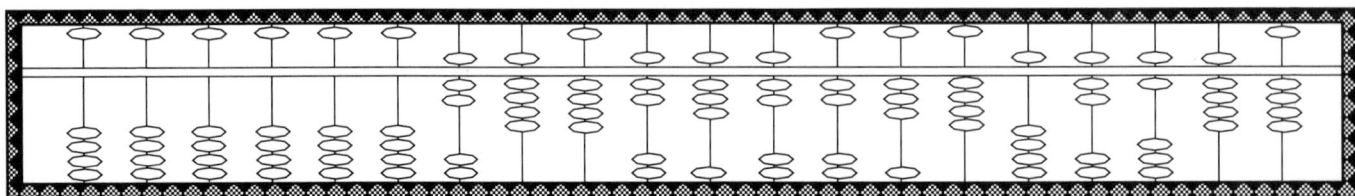

Napier's bones

Before the electronic calculator, almost every mathematics student would have used a set of logarithms. This was a book of tables which allowed a student to multiply very large numbers together by doing simple addition. These sets of logarithms were devised by a Scottish mathematician called John Napier (1550–1617). Another set of tables, also devised by Napier and known as Napier's bones, is shown opposite. The bones were used to do calculations that involved multiplying and dividing large numbers.

									Indicator strip
1	2	3	4	5	6	7	8	9	I
2	4	6	8	1/0	1/2	1/4	1/6	1/8	II
3	6	9	1/2	1/5	1/8	2/1	2/4	2/7	III
4	8	1/2	1/6	2/0	2/4	2/8	3/2	3/6	IV
5	1/0	1/5	2/0	2/5	3/0	3/5	4/0	4/5	V
6	1/2	1/8	2/4	3/0	3/6	4/2	4/8	5/4	VI
7	1/4	2/1	2/8	3/5	4/2	4/9	5/6	6/3	VII
8	1/6	2/4	3/2	4/0	4/8	5/6	6/4	7/2	VIII
9	1/8	2/7	3/6	4/5	5/4	6/3	7/2	8/1	IX

The example here shows how to use Napier's bones to multiply:

1548×43

The bones are used to do the four multiplications: 8×43, 40×43, 500×43 and 1000×43. The answers to these calculations are then added together to obtain the final answer.

4	3	I
8	6	II
1/2	9	III
1/6	1/2	IV
2/0	1/5	V
2/4	1/8	VI
2/8	2/1	VII
3/2	2/4	VIII
3/6	2/7	IX

Make a copy of the table and cut the columns into strips. Put the 4 and 3 strips together so that the top row reads '43', with the indicator strip beside them as shown.

Use row VIII to calculate 8×43. Add the numbers that fall with in the diagonal lines.

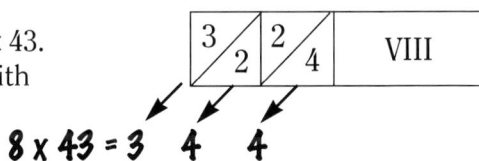

3/2	2/4	VIII

$$8 \times 43 = 3 \quad 4 \quad 4$$

Similarly, use row IV to calculate 4×43 and add a nought so that you have 40×43.

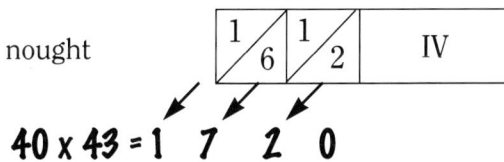

1/6	1/2	IV

$$40 \times 43 = 1 \quad 7 \quad 2 \quad 0$$

Row V will give you 500×43 and row I will give you 1000×43. Add the answers together:

```
                344
               1720
              21500
              43000
1548 × 43 =   66564
```

See if you can do these multiplications using Napier's bones.

2496 x 382 **11243 x 5432**
84 x 716 **9875 x 3143** **635 x 4157**

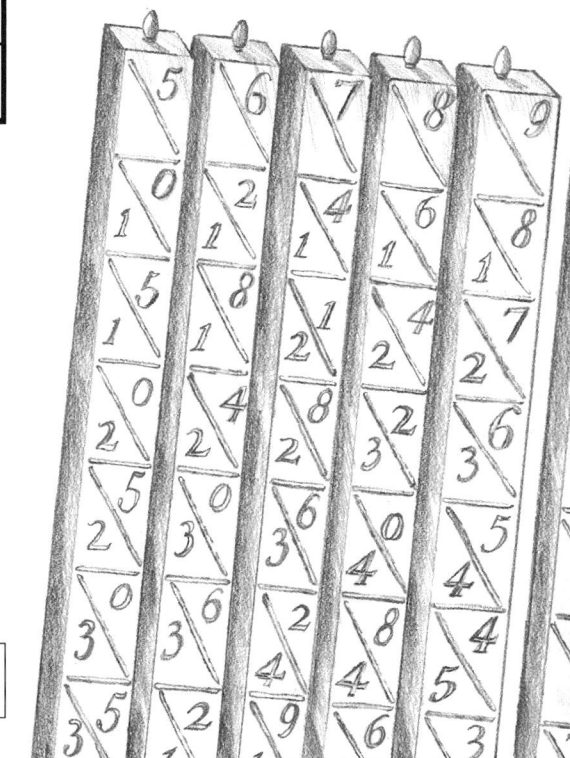

A number puzzle

2	1	9
4	3	8
6	5	7

There are many ways to arrange the digits 1 to 9 so that the first and second rows sum to the total of the third row. *How many ways can you find?*

A number of puzzles

'I was looking through the newspaper the other day when I came upon this curious advertisement...'

Each prize was to last for the winner's lifetime. These were the prizes offered:

(A) £2000 in the first year, £3900 (double less £100) in the second year, £7700 (double the previous year less £100) in the third year and so on.

(B) £1000 in the first year, £2500 (two and a half times the previous year's amount) in the second year, £6250 (two and a half times the previous year's amount) in the third year and so on.

(C) £100 in the first year, £200 (double the previous year) in the second year, £400 (double the previous year) in the third year and so on.

If you were lucky enough to throw six sixes which prize, A, B or C, would you choose?

A WORKING YEAR

TOM WAS THINKING ABOUT HIS JOB PROSPECTS...

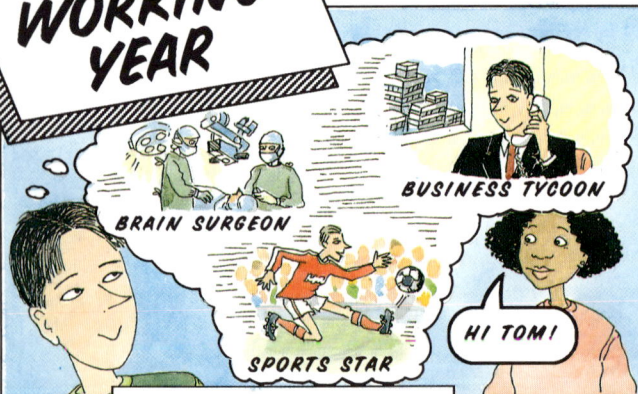

BRAIN SURGEON

BUSINESS TYCOON

SPORTS STAR

...WHEN ALONG CAME CLARE

HI TOM!

HI CLARE! I WAS JUST THINKING ABOUT WHEN I START MY FIRST JOB... £20000, £30000 A YEAR...

WELL, IF I WAS AN EMPLOYER, I WOULDN'T PAY YOU A PENNY.

WHY?

THERE ARE 365 DAYS IN A YEAR. YOU SLEEP 8 HOURS A DAY. THAT MAKES 122 DAYS

YOU SPEND 8 HOURS A DAY AT LEISURE, WATCHING TV, READING, EATING AND SO ON

WHICH LEAVES 121 DAYS TO DO SOME WORK IN. YOU HAVE 52 SATURDAYS AND 52 SUNDAYS OFF, THAT LEAVES 17 DAYS

HUH?!

YOU WANT HALF A HOUR EACH DAY FOR LUNCH, THAT'S 5 DAYS... WHICH LEAVES 12 WORKING DAYS

YOU EXPECT 2 WEEKS ANNUAL HOLIDAY, THAT MAKES 10 WORKING DAYS... LEAVING 2 DAYS FOR CHRISTMAS AND NEW YEAR... THAT LEAVES 0 DAYS!

WHAT IS WRONG WITH CLARE'S ADDING UP?

16

Profit or loss

Kate bought two rare stamps for her collection. A year later she sold them for £6000 each. Kate made a profit of 20% on one stamp and a loss of 20% on the other. *Did Kate make a profit or loss overall on the sale of the two stamps?*

One is light

There were 24 gold coins in the bag but not all were made of solid gold. One of the coins had been mixed with another metal and weighed one gram less than a solid gold one. *Using a pair of pan-scales, like the ones below, what is the minimum number of weighings needed to discover the light coin?*

MISSING DIME?

IN THE PIZZA PARADE, JUST OFF SIXTH AVENUE, ENRICO SERVED THE LAST CUSTOMERS OF THE DAY.

WE'LL EACH HAVE A SPICY PIZZA AND A COFFEE, PLEASE

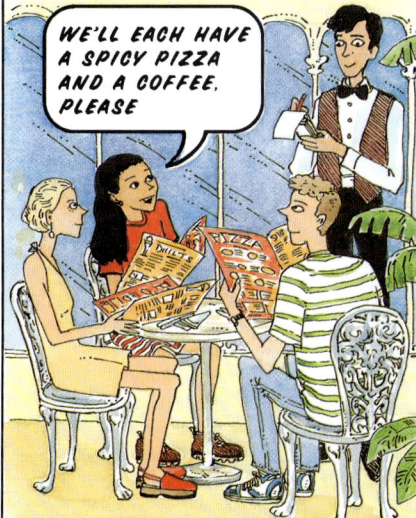

THEY WERE A GROUP OF THREE. ENRICO HANDED THEM THE BILL.

THAT WILL BE $3 EACH

THE GROUP HANDED OVER $3 EACH. ENRICO TOOK THE MONEY TO THE COUNTER

AT THE COUNTER

EH! ENRICO. SPICY IS ON SPECIAL OFFER TODAY. THEY'VE OVERPAID BY 50 CENTS. GIVE THIS BACK TO THEM.

ON HIS WAY BACK TO THE TABLE, ENRICO THOUGHT TO HIMSELF...

I CAN'T DIVIDE THE 5 COINS BETWEEN THREE. I KNOW. I'LL GIVE THEM 10 CENTS EACH AND KEEP THE REST AS A TIP.

THAT NIGHT ENRICO WAS LYING IN BED THINKING...

... THEY EACH HAD A 10 CENT REBATE, WHICH MEANS THEY PAID $2.90 EACH. THAT ADDS UP TO $8.70. I HAD 20 CENTS - THAT MAKES $8.90 - SO WHERE DID THE OTHER 10 CENTS GO?

CAN YOU FIND THE MISSING DIME?

17

Cryptarithms

The word cryptarithm was coined in 1931 in a Belgian mathematical magazine. The puzzle opposite accompanied an article which said that ... 'in cryptology numbers are usually substituted for letters. In a cryptarithm it is the other way round ...' *Can you crack the code?*

$$\begin{array}{r} ABC \\ \times\ DE \\ \hline FEC \\ DEC \\ \hline HGBC \end{array}$$

Cracking cryptarithms

Though cryptarithms were not given a name until 1931, they have been around for a long time. It is possible to solve them without doing much arithmetic. Cryptarithms have certain conventions, that is rules which are accepted by most people who make them up or solve them.

Each letter stands for a different digit between 0 and 9. Here is an example; what can we deduce?

$$\begin{array}{r} BAG \\ \times\ GAB \\ \hline A\bullet\bullet \\ \bullet\bullet B \\ \bullet B\bullet \\ \hline \bullet G\bullet\bullet\bullet \end{array}$$

None of the digits can be 0 or 1 because digits have changed place in all three products.

None of the digits can be over 4 or some of the products would be more than 3 digits. So the three digits possible are 2, 3 and 4.

B cannot be a number greater than 3. If B were 4 then the product of BAG × B would consist of more than 3 digits.

Therefore, B is either 2 or 3.

G × A = B, so neither G nor A can be 2.

Therefore, B is 2.

Can you deduce any more? Can you complete the multiplication?

Sometimes you need to use a combination of deduction and trial and error to solve the cryptarithm.

Can you put two numbers made from one each of the ten digits (1234567890) to replace the spots to make a multiplication sum? Zero is not to be at the start or end of either number.

$$\begin{array}{r} \bullet\bullet\bullet\bullet\bullet\bullet\bullet\bullet\bullet\bullet \\ \times\ 2 \\ \hline \bullet\bullet\bullet\bullet\bullet\bullet\bullet\bullet\bullet\bullet \end{array}$$

$$\begin{array}{r} SEND \\ + MORE \\ \hline MONEY \end{array} \qquad \begin{array}{r} TEN \\ TEN \\ + FORTY \\ \hline SIXTY \end{array}$$

There is no zero in the following two cryptarithms.

$$\begin{array}{r} WRONG \\ + WRONG \\ \hline RIGHT \end{array} \qquad \begin{array}{r} SEAM \\ \times\ \ T \\ \hline MEATS \end{array}$$

E is zero, 1 and 6 are not used in this cryptarithm. The letters stand for different digits. The dots stand for a digit that only shows up in the product.

$$\begin{array}{r} GREEN \\ \times\ RED \\ \hline \bullet\bullet ORANGE \end{array}$$

Cryptarithmetic game

This is a game for two players, using the letters of the alphabet A to J and the numbers one to ten. You will need pencils and paper.

Each player takes it in turn to devise the code to be used. Player One devises a code using the first 10 letters of the alphabet and keeps it hidden from Player Two. For example:

1	2	3	4	5	6	7	8	9	0
F	C	G	J	H	E	I	A	D	B

Player Two makes up sums using the letters:

G + H

and Player One gives the answer (in code):

G + H = A

Player Two continues to make up sums using letters until the code is cracked.

Then the players swop roles.

What strategies should you use to find out as quickly as possible what each letter stands for?

Arranging numbers

Can you rearrange the numbers in this wheel so that three numbers in a line always add up to 30?

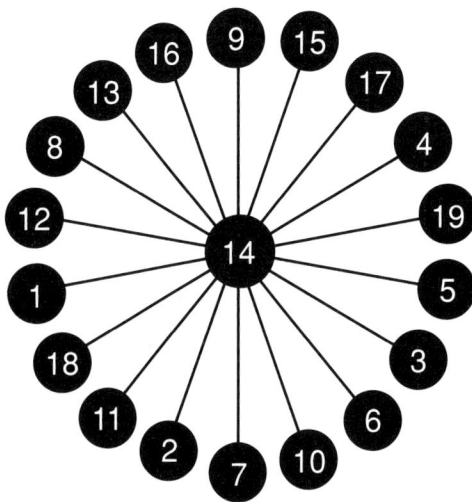

Can you rearrange the numbers in the squares so that all the sums are correct?

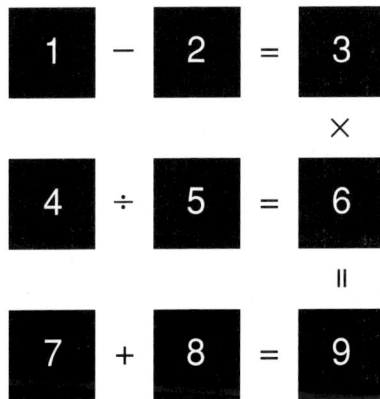

$$1 - 2 = 3$$
$$\times$$
$$4 \div 5 = 6$$
$$=$$
$$7 + 8 = 9$$

Can you rearrange the numbers so that the three sides each add up to 20?

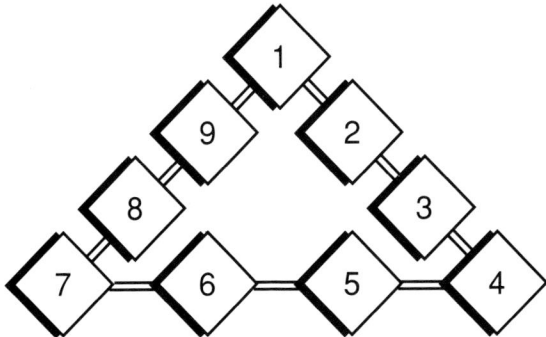

19

The Chinese Triangle

The number triangle above appeared in 1303 in a Chinese book by Chu Shih Chieh, called *The Precious Mirror of the Fair Elements*. The symbols represent numbers. By looking at the first few rows of the triangle you should be able to see how the triangle is made and what number each of the Chinese symbols represents. It would then be possible to carry on with the triangle for many more rows.

There are many interesting number patterns within this triangle. They can be found by looking along different lines of numbers as shown opposite.

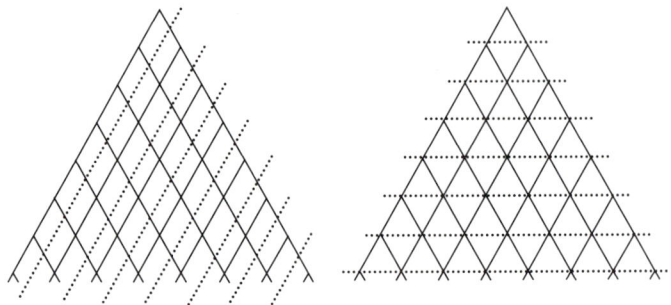

It is also possible to create geometric patterns using the triangle as a basis for determining different colouring arrangements. The pattern below is created by fitting together six of the number triangles which have been made by using the modulo 3 system for addition, as described underneath.

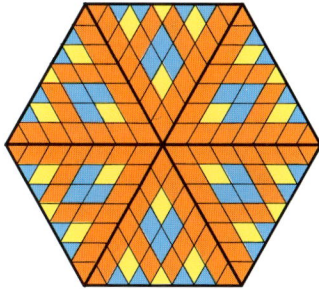

In modulo 3 you use a clock with 0, 1 and 2 on the face. Only the digits 0, 1 and 2 are used. For example:

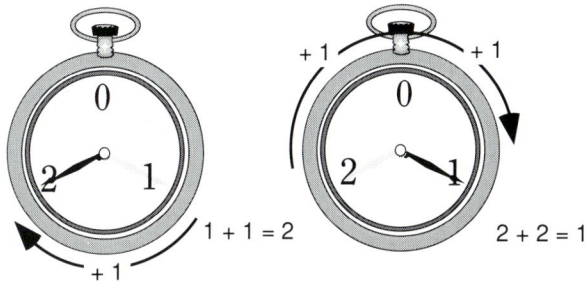

$1 + 1 = 2$

$2 + 2 = 1$

So:

$0 + 1 = 1$	$1 + 1 = 2$	$2 + 1 = 0$
$0 + 2 = 2$	$1 + 2 = 0$	$2 + 2 = 1$

The triangle below is created using addition in modulo 3. Once the numbers have been found each number is given a different colour. The coloured triangle is then used to make the hexagon.

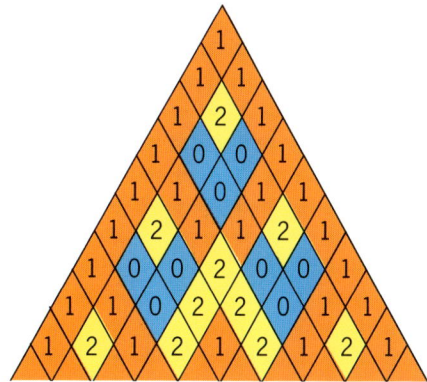

Different patterns can be created by using different modulo systems for adding together the numbers. It would also be possible to use different starting numbers in the top of the pattern, or use a different generating rule to create the numbers.
Investigate these different triangles.

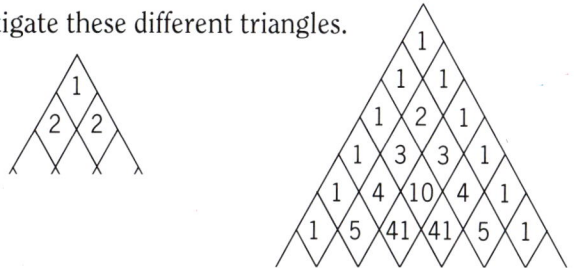

The Indian Triangle

The triangle also appeared in India in the 10th century. It was known as the *meruprastara* and was drawn out by a person called Halayudha. The *meruprastara* was used to work out the number of ways short and long sounds could be combined together in poetic rhythms of different lengths.

You can make up your own music in a similar way. Instead of thinking about a long and short sound the following idea is based on either making a sound or having a rest. Decide whether you will make your sound with your voice or with a musical instrument. Decide how long you want your line to be and then work out how many different combinations there would be for putting the sounds and the rests together. For example, if your line is going to be 3 beats long then you could arrange your sounds as follows:

beat	beat	beat
beat	beat	rest
beat	rest	beat
rest	beat	beat

rest	rest	rest
rest	rest	beat
rest	beat	rest
beat	rest	rest

If a group of you play several lines together repeatedly you can make some interesting rhythms. For example, person A could play beat rest beat, beat rest beat, beat rest beat, at the same time as person B plays rest beat beat, rest beat beat, rest beat beat, and so on. You could create more variations by using different instruments.

Create different rhythms by looking at the combinations possible in a 4-beat line. *Can you see how the meruprastara helped with calculating how many different combinations there were?*

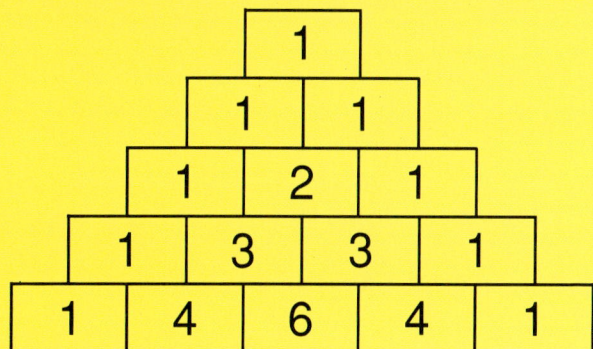

Why do they work?

'I need half an hour to get through this marking,' thought the teacher to himself. 'I know, I shall set them an addition problem to keep them quiet.'

'I want you to sum all the numbers 1 to 1000,' said the teacher to the class.

In less than a minute the hand of Carl Gauss shot up. 'I've got the answer!' he cried. And he had, without using his slate. Carl Gauss went on to become a very distinguished mathematician. His method for solving this problem was quite straightforward.

How did Carl do it?
Well, he worked out that $1 + 999 = 1000$, $2 + 998 = 1000$, $3 + 997 = 1000$ ... and so on.

Try summing all the numbers 1 to 10. *Do you notice anything?* Try summing 1 to 50, 1 to 100. *What is the sum of all the numbers 1 to 1000?*

Given any number series where the difference between two numbers next to each other is always the same, how could you add up all the numbers from the first to the last term?

THE ANSWER IS...

$$0 + 1000 = 1000$$
$$1 + 999 = 1000$$
$$2 + 998 = 1000$$
$$3 + 997 = 1000$$

Fast add
Ask a friend to give you a 4-digit number and write it down. **2410**

Write your own 4-digit number under it. **7589**

Ask your friend for another 4-digit number and write it down. **6823**

Again write your own 4-digit number. **3176**

Ask your friend for a final 4-digit number. **5522**

25520

Offer your friend a calculator and challenge her to add the numbers before you can do it in your head. Here's how to beat her. Write 2 followed by the last 4-digit number written after subtracting 2 from it. (If the last digit was 0 it is a little more difficult.)

Can you see how it works? Try adding together single digits in the same column in the first two rows. *Why do you add and subtract 2?*

1 to 31
What day of the month were you born on? Look at the cards below. Select the cards the date appears on. Now add together the numbers in the top left column and that is your birthday. Think of another number between 1 and 31 and see if it works again. Try it on a friend.

A		B		C		D		E	
8	24	16	24	2	18	4	20	1	17
9	25	17	25	3	19	5	21	3	19
10	26	18	26	6	22	6	22	5	21
11	27	19	27	7	23	7	23	7	23
12	28	20	28	10	26	12	28	9	25
13	29	21	29	11	27	13	29	11	27
14	30	22	30	14	30	14	30	13	29
15	31	23	31	15	31	15	31	15	31

A clue to figuring out how this works is that it involves changing numbers into base 2.

1001 trick

PUT ANY 3-DIGIT NUMBER INTO YOUR CALCULATOR.

921

REPEAT THE NUMBER TO MAKE IT 6-DIGITS LONG.

921921

DIVIDE THIS NUMBER BY 13...

70917

... NOW DIVIDE THIS NUMBER BY 11...

6447

... FINALLY DIVIDE THIS NUMBER BY 7. WHAT DO YOU GET?

IT'S THE NUMBER I STARTED WITH! DOES IT WORK FOR ANY 3-DIGIT NUMBER?

TRY IT!

How does it work?

The 6-digit number you get when you repeat the 3-digit number is the same total you would get if you multiplied the 3-digit number by 1001.

$$
\begin{array}{r}
921 \\
\times\ 1001 \\
\hline
921000 \\
921 \\
\hline
921921
\end{array}
$$

1001 has only 3 prime factors, that is prime numbers that it can be divided by without leaving a remainder. They are 13, 11 and 7.

Try multiplying $7 \times 11 \times 13$. *What do you get?*

Try multiplying $921 \times 7 \times 11 \times 13$. *What do you get?*

When you divide your 6-digit number by 13, 11 and 7 you are just doing the reverse process.

Multiply the Russian way

In the last century, a method of multiplication which involved only doubling and halving was very popular in Russia. This is how it worked:

Take two numbers ... say, 26×48.

Put the largest number in the left-hand column. Halve the first number and double the second. Carry on repeating this until the first number gets to 1.

If in the halving you get a fraction go to the next whole number below it.

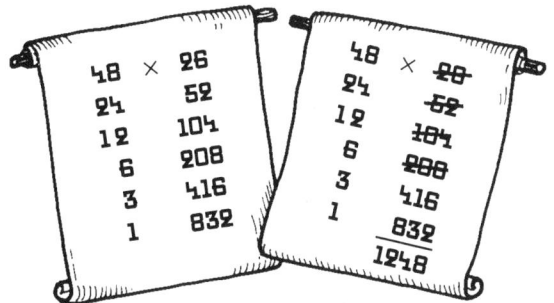

48	×	26
24		52
12		104
6		208
3		416
1		832

48	×	26
24		52
12		104
6		208
3		416
1		832
		1248

Cross out all the numbers in the right-hand column that are opposite an even number in the left-hand column. To get the answer add the remaining numbers in the right-hand column.

Can you do these multiplications the Russian way?

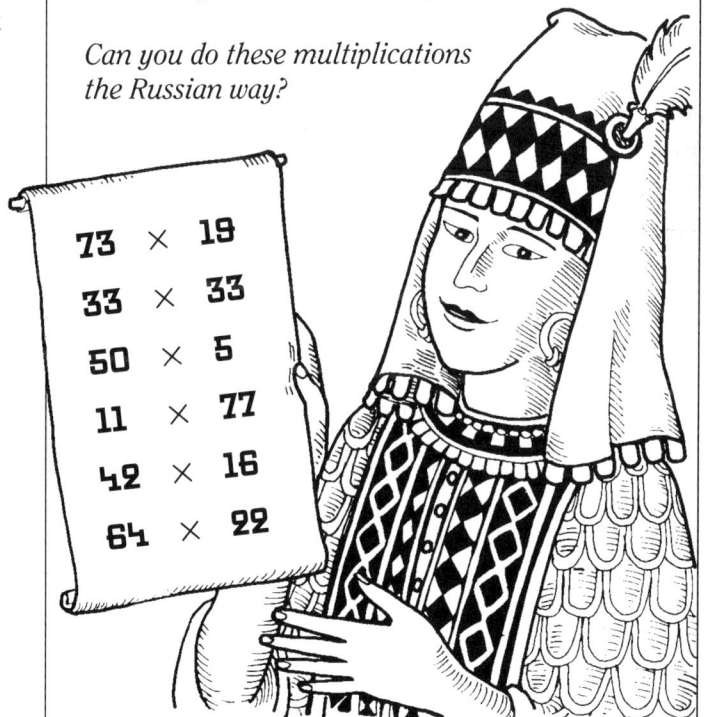

73	×	19
33	×	33
50	×	5
11	×	77
42	×	16
64	×	22

Can you multiply a 3-digit number this way?

How many ways?

Mathematical problems can often be expressed in a number of different ways, which may lead to different questions being asked.

How many different squares can you see in each of these patterns as they grow bigger?

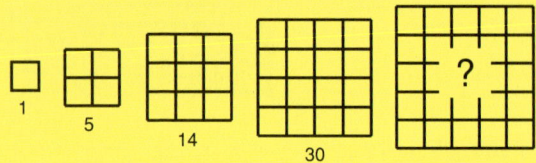

1 5 14 30 ?

How many different triangles can you see in each of these patterns as they grow bigger?

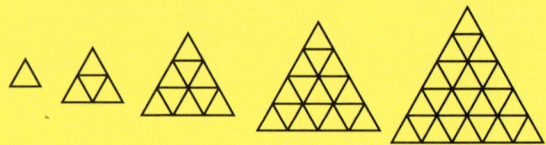

How many different rhombuses can you see in each of these patterns as they grow bigger?

Is it possible to work out the next number in the sequence without drawing the shape?

Is it possible to work out any number in the sequence without drawing the shape?

Designs from a Chinese lattice

Other questions about counting 'how many' involve the puzzler looking for different solutions and checking that they haven't missed any possibilities out, or found 'repeat' or 'duplicate' solutions.

Try making this Chinese lattice design.

Start with a tessellation of regular hexagons.

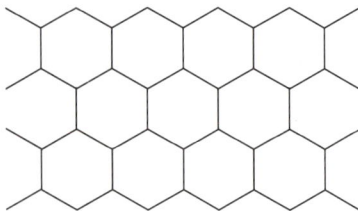

Join up the mid-point of each hexagon to the mid-point of the hexagon touching it

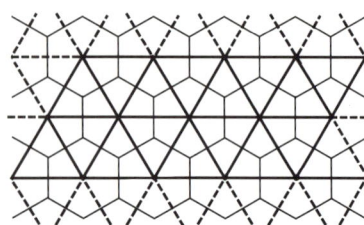

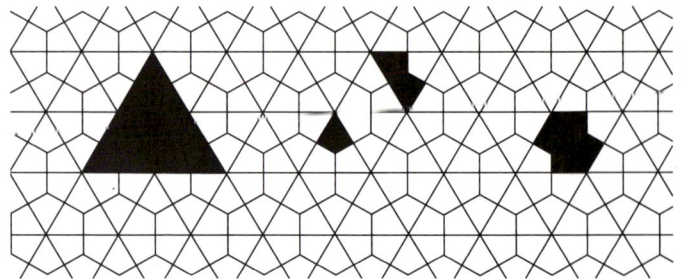

Make some copies of this Chinese lattice design. Shade in different areas on the design. *How many shapes can you find with just one line of symmetry? How about two or three lines of symmetry? Does the shape you have found have rotational symmetry?*

Can you find shapes that tessellate?

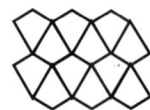

For each question, how will you know if you have found all the possible solutions or if there is a finite number of solutions?

In addition to counting the ways, more mathematics may be involved in deciding whether one way is different from another way you have found. It is not necessarily clear as you search for your solutions.

In the following two problems you may well create 'replicas' (identical patterns) when you are searching for the different number of ways possible in each idea. In these cases you will need to decide on a method for checking for repeats.

Polygons into triangles

Use regular polygons. By drawing lines from corner to corner find out how many ways you can cut the polygon up into triangles. (You are not allowed to draw the lines across other lines in this problem.)

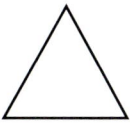

0 lines can be drawn from corner to corner so there are 0 ways to cut this shape into different triangles.

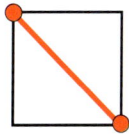

1 line can be drawn from corner to corner. So there is 1 way to cut this shape into triangles.

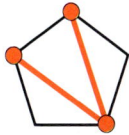

2 lines can be drawn from corner to corner and there is one way to cut this shape into triangles.

You can use 3 lines drawn from corner to corner in the hexagon.

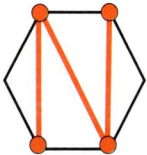

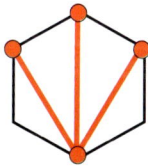

There are 3 ways to cut the hexagon into triangles.

Colouring corners of polygons

Imagine you are going to colour the corners of each of the regular polygons using two colours. How many ways can you colour the corners of the polygons so that each arrangement of colours is different?

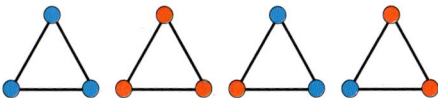

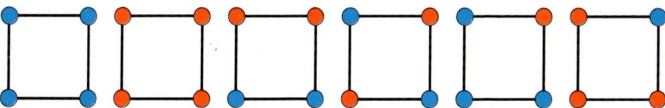

Spy lights

A spy stationed on an island worked out a way of sending messages to her accomplice on the mainland during the darkness of night. She fixed six hooks to her attic window and from these she could hang three lamps.

The battery powered lamps could have inter-changeable clear (white), red or green lenses put in them. She had enough of each lens to hang all three lamps in one colour.

By using the red, green or clear lenses in the lamps and hanging either 1, 2 or 3 lamps in different positions on the hooks, how many different signals could be sent?

Note that from a distance two white lamps placed on hooks 2 and 4 would look the same as two white lamps placed on hooks 3 and 5.

Will the spy encounter any other problems with her system?

Arabian mathematics

Lattice multiplication
The Arabs developed a way of multiplying called the 'lattice' method. This is how it works.

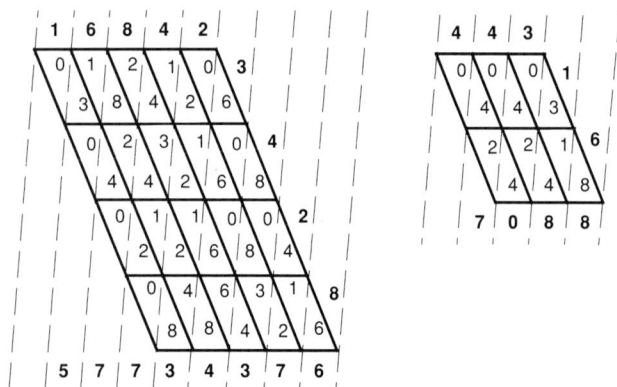

Lay out the numbers to be multiplied along the top and down the right-hand side. You make small multiplications to fill the cells. *Can you see how?* To get the product of the two numbers you add the numbers on the diagonal – carrying over when necessary. The number of cells needed depends on the lengths of the numbers that are being multiplied together. Trace over the grids and try to do these multiplications.

8964 × 73   **56482 × 16**
7286 × 253   **764 × 764**

Casting out nines
This is a method that was used in India to check that an answer to a large multiplication was correct. This is how it works for $16\,842 \times 3428 = 57\,734\,376$.

Sum, separately, all the digits in the two numbers multiplied and divide by 9.
$1 + 6 + 8 + 4 + 2 = 21 \div 9 = 2$ r3
$3 + 4 + 2 + 8 = 17 \div 9 = 1$ r8   (r means remainder)

Multiply the remainders together and then add the digits of the answer.
$3 \times 8 = 24$ $2 + 4 = 6$

Now sum the digits of the answer to the multiplication and divide by 9.
$5 + 7 + 7 + 3 + 4 + 3 + 7 + 6 = 42 \div 9 = 4$ r6

If the two remainders are the same, 6 in this case, then the multiplication is probably correct. *(Can you think why it might not be?)* If the two answers are not the same then your multiplication is definitely wrong.

Mathematics is always developing
The development of mathematics has taken place over the centuries and each civilisation across the world has played an important part in its development. New ideas are discovered by mathematicians and ideas from previous times and different civilisations are explored and developed further. The Arabians made contributions to many aspects of mathematics, including the theory of numbers, the development of algebra and trigonometry. Much of the work undertaken in the 7th to 11th centuries AD is recognisable in the mathematics that we learn today.

Algebra
The word *Algebra* is said to have come from the word *al-jabr* which was used by Arabian mathematicians to mean 'adding equal quantities to both sides of an equation to get rid of any negative quantities', or subtracting equal quantities from both sides in order to come closer to a solution. Here are two examples.

A quantity take away 7 equals 5

$$x - 7 = 5$$
$$x - 7 + 5 = 5 + 7$$
$$x = 12$$

A quantity added to 4 equals 23

$$x + 4 = 23$$
$$x + 4 - 4 = 23 - 4$$
$$x = 19$$

It was also used to describe the way you multiply both sides of an equation to get rid of fractional quantities.

Half of a quantity equals 12

$$\tfrac{1}{2}x = 12$$
$$\tfrac{1}{2}x \times 2 = 12 \times 2$$
$$x = 24$$

The word *al-mugabala* was used to describe the way that you collect like terms together before reducing the terms further. For example:

Nine subtracted from eight times a quantity equals twice that quantity.

$$8x - 9 = 2x$$
$$8x - 2x - 9 = 2x - 2x$$
$$6x - 9 = 0$$
$$6x - 9 - 9 = 0 + 9$$
$$6x = 9$$
$$\frac{6x}{6} = \frac{9}{6}$$
$$x = 1\tfrac{3}{6} \text{ or } 1\tfrac{1}{2}$$

A mathematician called Musa al-Khwarizmi wrote books on algebra, arithmetic, astronomy and geography. His book on algebra called *Hisab al-jabr w'al-mugabala* was written in the 9th century. The last part of the book was devoted to solving some algebraic problems about numbers. Arabs would call the unknown number *the thing* or *the root of a plant* and all the quantities in the equations are numbers. Many of the problems were quite difficult, for example:

A number is multiplied by itself. The result is added to 8. On subtracting 6 times the original number, nothing is left. *What is the number?* (There are two possible answers.)

It is possible to find the answers by trial and error, but it could take a long time.

The problems below are fairly straightforward. Try using algebra to see how quickly you can do them.

Added to 3
A quantity added to three is equal to seven. *What is that quantity?*

Four times
Four times a quantity added to seven is equal to twenty-three. *What is that quantity?*

Seven times
Seven times a quantity added to five is equal to twice that quantity added to thirty. *What is that quantity?*

Below are some interesting algebraic problems, written in words. These are not as straightforward as the previous three. *Can you solve them?*

You can check to see if you are right by going through the algebra with your answers in. Make up your own problems and use algebra to solve them.

How old?
A daughter is exactly one-third the age of her mother and she has a sister who is one-sixth of her own age. The ages of all three amount to 50 years. *How old are each of them?*

Mother and son
A mother's and son's ages add together to make 80 years. If you double the son's age it is greater than the mother's age by 10 years. *How old are the mother and son?*

Red and green
There are two types of counters in a bag. There are three times as many red counters as there are green counters. When four red counters and four green counters are removed from the bag there are four times as many red counters as there are green counters. *How many red counters were there in the bag in the first place?*

Differ by one
Find two numbers in the ratio of 4 to 5, so that if you add 6 to the larger number and 1 to the smaller number the square roots of the new numbers will differ from each other by 1.

20 more
If you multiply two numbers together the answer is 180. If you increase the smaller of the two numbers by one and then multiply the two numbers together the new answer will be 20 more than the first answer. *What are the numbers?*

Number shapes

Every whole number can be made with:
1 triangle number or
2 triangle numbers added together or
3 triangle numbers added together.

Some whole numbers can be made in more than one of these ways. After three, at least one branch must have more than one apple. The triangular orchard above shows how this works. How would the orchard grow for the next ten whole numbers?

WE COULD PUT ALL THE CRYSTALS INTO A SQUARE BASED PYRAMID

WE COULD PUT THEM INTO A TRIANGULAR BASED PYRAMID

Is it possible to make these pyramids with a square number of crystals?

Cube statues

These statues are made by sticking cubes together. *How many for the size 3 cube? How many for the size 10 cube? If the cubes were completely hollow and were only made made up of the smaller cubes on the outside layer, how many cubes would be needed for each size cube?*

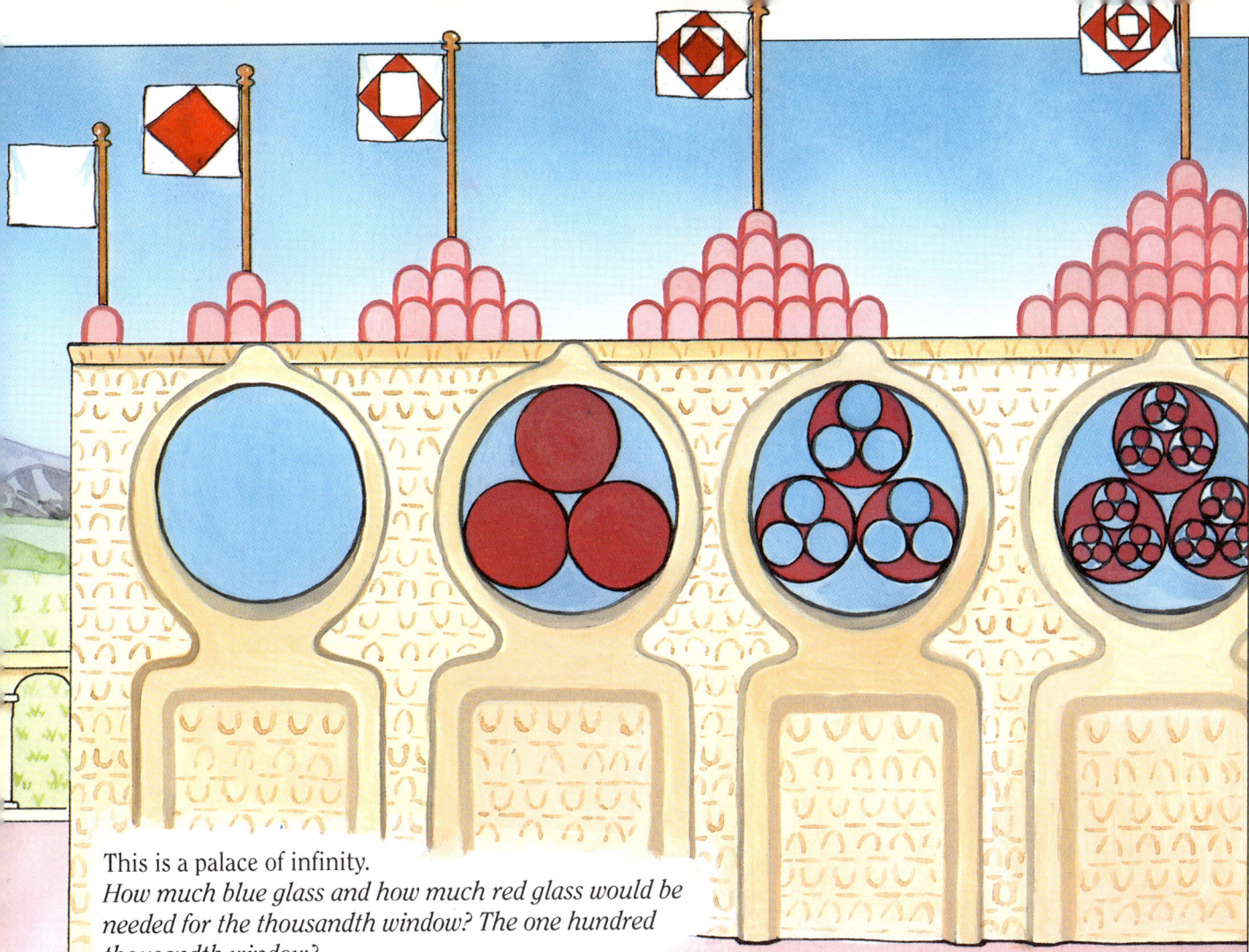

This is a palace of infinity.
How much blue glass and how much red glass would be needed for the thousandth window? The one hundred thousandth window? ...

Each turret roof has the same number of tiles on each of its four sides. *How many roof tiles on the tenth turret? The hundredth? The thousandth?*

This path continues to the right. Can you work out the pattern? *How many different arrangements are there for a 5-tile pavement, a 6-tile pavement ...?*

There is a flag on each turret. *How much of the sixth flag will be coloured red?*

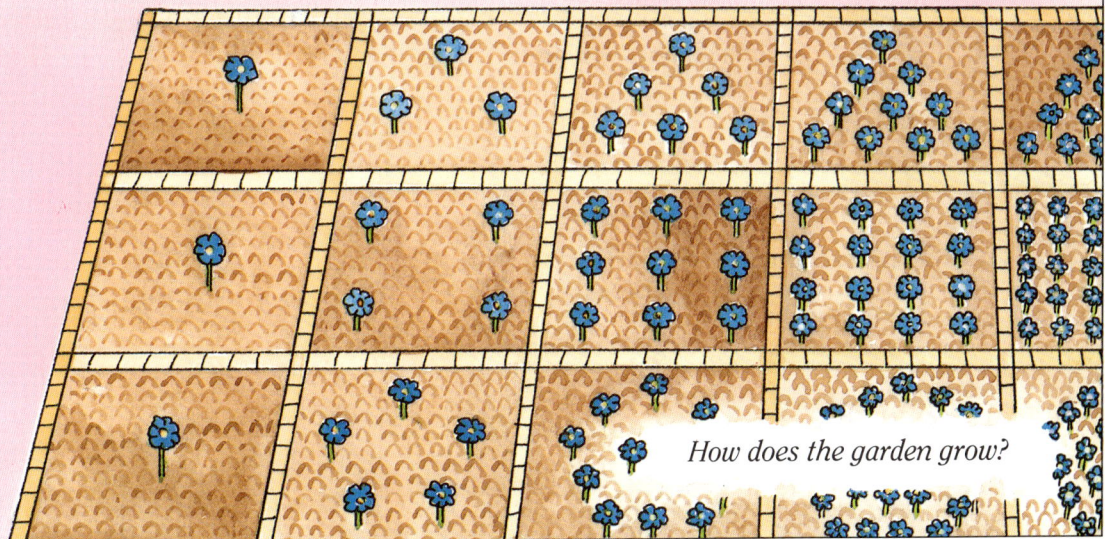

How does the garden grow?

A page of π

Finding π (approximately 3.142)

How do you 'measure' π? Use a tape measure or a piece of string, as described below. Find a number of different-sized circular objects such as tin cans, plates, waste bin.

Use a ruler to measure the diameter of each of the objects and write the results down.

	DIAMETER
CAN	
BIN	
PLATE	
BIG CAN	

Now measure around the circular object or find some string and wind it once around the object.

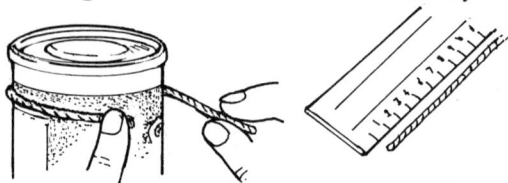

Unwind but keep careful hold of where the string meets. Measure the length of the string with your ruler and write down the results in a table.

	DIAMETER	CIRCUMFERENCE	C÷D
CAN			
BIN			
PLATE			
BIG CAN			

Now divide the circumference of each object by its diameter. Look at the results – *what do you notice?*

Find some more circular objects. Measure their diameter. *Can you predict their circumference?* You can check your prediction by measuring.

Pi (π) has puzzled mathematicians throughout the ages. It is a special type of irrational number called a *transcendental* number. This means that, unlike all decimal fractions, it will continue without ever repeating in a pattern and without ever coming to an end. Therefore π can never be written down exactly.

Throughout history, mathematicians have spent time trying to calculate π to an ever-increasing number of decimal places. The Ancient Egyptians, Hebrews and early Chinese used the value 3.

More accurate values of π than 3 were needed when machinery based on the wheel began to come into use. For example, Archimedes, an Ancient Greek mathematician, invented a method for launching ships using cogs and his invention of an irrigation pump was based on the rotation of a screw.

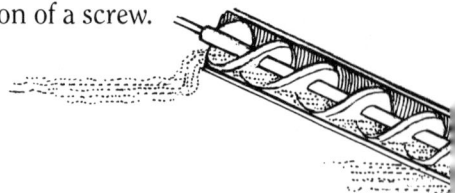

Archimedes drew regular polygons inside circles (inscribed) and outside circles (circumscribed) to get approximations of π. The more sides the polygon had the closer would be Archimedes' approximation.

Archimedes' method

Keep the radius of the circle equal to 1 and then the area of the circle, which is πr^2, will be equal to π.

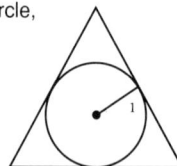

The area of the circle is bigger than the inscribed triangle but smaller than the circumscribed triangle.

The area of the circle is bigger than the inscribed square but smaller than the circumscribed square.

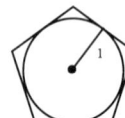

The area of the circle is bigger than the inscribed pentagon but smaller than the circumscribed pentagon.

By using regular polygons with 96 sides, Archimedes showed that π was larger than $3\frac{10}{71}$ but smaller than $3\frac{1}{7}$.

Although mathematicians have calculated π to a large number of places it is very unlikely that the number will ever need to be used with that degree of accuracy. As Simon Newcomb, an American astronomer and mathematician, wrote:

Ten decimal places are sufficient to give the circumference of the Earth to the fraction of an inch, and thirty decimal places would give the circumference of the whole visible universe to a quantity imperceptible with the most powerful telescope.

π occurs in other places. It is used by actuaries in a formula to calculate the number of people left alive in a given group of people after a certain number of years.

Mathematicians have also calculated π by creating formulae which will give an approximation to π. As the series grows, the answer gets closer to π.

Lord Brouncker (1620–1684)

$$\pi = \cfrac{4}{1 + \cfrac{1^2}{2 + \cfrac{3^2}{2 + \cfrac{5^2}{2 + 7^2}}}}$$
...

John Wallis (1616–1703)

$$\frac{\pi}{2} = \frac{2}{1} \times \frac{2}{3} \times \frac{4}{3} \times \frac{4}{5} \times \frac{6}{5} \times \frac{6}{7} \times \frac{8}{7} \times \frac{8}{9} \times ...$$

Leibniz (1646–1716)

$$\frac{\pi}{4} = 1 - \frac{1}{3} + \frac{1}{5} - \frac{1}{7} + \frac{1}{9} - \frac{1}{11} + \frac{1}{13} - \frac{1}{15} + ...$$

Matching π

The following experiment will give you a number which is approximately equal to π.

Use some headless matches. On a piece of paper draw some parallel lines which are double the distance apart as the matches are long. Hold the matchsticks about 30 cm above the paper and drop them one by one. Count the number of matches that have either touched or crossed a line.

When you have finished making the drops do the following calculation:

(Total number of matches dropped) ÷ (Total number of matches crossing or touching line)

Matchsticks must be half the length of the distance between the lines.

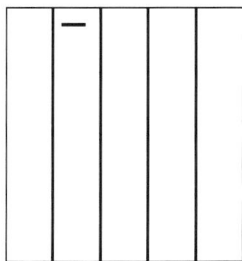

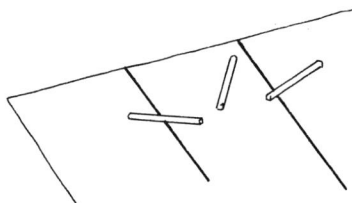

The more times you drop the matches the more likely it is that your result will be close to π.

Some puzzling circles

Floating island
A family of seals inhabits this circular island of ice. After a family row they agree to divide the ice island into two identical pieces with the same number of seals on each part as they are positioned now. *How did they do it?*

A magic circle
A magician placed 10 penguins into a magic circle as below. She then drew 3 more magic circles inside the large one so that if none of the penguins crossed any of the magic lines they would each have their own compartments. *Where did she draw her circles?*

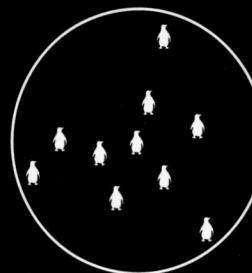

Further ways

Arranging cans

In mathematics arranging the same items in different ways is called permutations. Take three cans of paint. *How many different ways can they be arranged?*

If there was only one can there would be only one arrangement.

With two cans ...

With three cans ...

How many ways for four cans? Five cans?

Number of ways of arranging three cans = $1 \times 2 \times 3 = 3!$

The sum above is a factorial. 3! means multiply together successive terms from one to the number which is followed by the exclamation mark. *Can the number of arrangements of 4 and 5 cans also be calculated like this?*

The Mathematician's Tale

One April night, 'twas windy and wet,
In the Tabard Inn ten pilgrims met.
Said our host, "We need a tale,
From the Mathematician, while we sup our ale,
Be quick, tell us a puzzle of mirth and fun."
"By St Nicholas," came the reply, "it shall be done."

And so with courteous manner and good cheer,
The Mathematician's tale began, as you shall hear.

"Once, long ago, ten knights did meet,
To sing and talk, to drink and eat,
But, alas it was, they came to disagree,
Of who sat where, next to thou or thee.
One knight drew his sword, and then another,
And each brother knight then slew each other.
The room was soon dark, coloured red,
As ten foolish knights lay dying or dead.
That night upon them a curse was lain,
That only arithmetic could explain.

Eating out

The café offers a choice of five starters, eight main courses and four puddings. You dine there each day on a three course meal. Every day you have a different meal. *If the café opened on 1 March, on what date would you have had all the possible combinations of meals?*

Alphabet

How many different arrangements of all the letters of the alphabet can be made? You may use each letter only once in each arrangement.

AB, AC, AD, AE, ...

Arranging fences

In a certain city square there stood 16 statues within a low wall arranged as in the grid below. Every year the mayor of the city places 9 movable fences so as to divide the statues into different size groups. In the arrangement below the statues are divided into groups of 8, 3, 3 and 2. This year the mayor wants to arrange the statues into groups of 6, 6 and 4. *Can he do it by moving only 2 fences? 3 fences? 4 fences? 5 fences? 6 fences? 7 fences?*

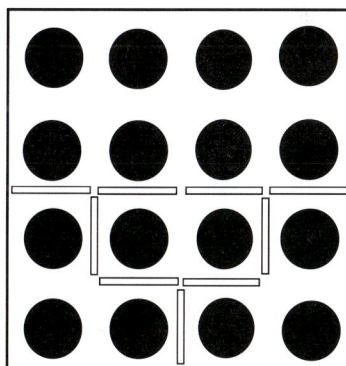

At this point the mathematician drew breath,
We all called out, "Tell us of their after-death!"

"The ghosts were to meet each year to dine,
And sit in different positions each time,
All the variations must they make,
Unless they could predict the number it take.
For only when the answer could be found,
Could the ten knights be heavenly bound."

The actuary declared, "To my mind then,
The knights could move from one to ten."
"No," said our host, "with ten people at table,
At least a hundred times are able."
"Far more, I think," said the good nun,
"It is an even greater sum!"

Now this puzzle I put to you,
How many permutations are possible to do?

Base two

There are 1100100 pennies in a pound!
This is how a computer would count them.

We do our calculations in the decimal system, which uses base ten.
Computers work with the binary system and use base two. In base two all
numbers can be represented using 0 and 1. In base 10, each new column is
the next power of ten; in base 2, each new column is the next power of 2.

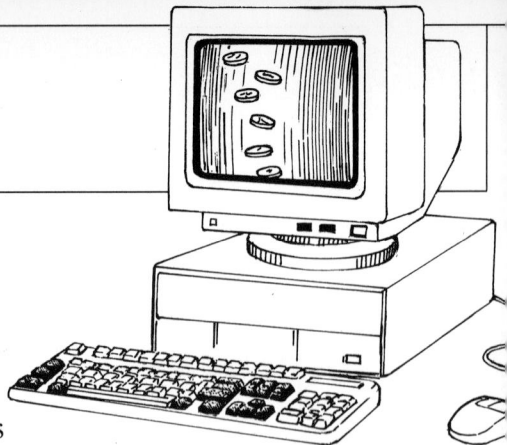

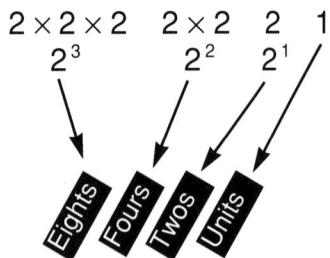

$$2 \times 2 \times 2 \quad 2 \times 2 \quad 2 \quad 1$$
$$2^3 \qquad\quad 2^2 \quad 2^1$$

Eights | Fours | Twos | Units

The number 47 would be written 101111.

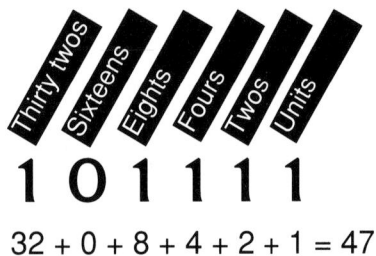

Thirty twos | Sixteens | Eights | Fours | Twos | Units

1 0 1 1 1 1

32 + 0 + 8 + 4 + 2 + 1 = 47

The number 117 would be written 1110111.

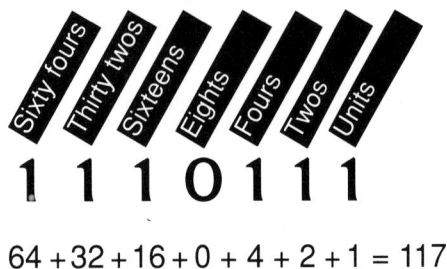

Sixty fours | Thirty twos | Sixteens | Eights | Fours | Twos | Units

1 1 1 0 1 1 1

64 + 32 + 16 + 0 + 4 + 2 + 1 = 117

Can you translate these binary numbers into decimal numbers?

11110110   111011

1011100000

1001101   1100000

1101000

Which base?

Base 2 is the most commonly used base other
than 10. But other bases can be used. Each pair of
dice add up to seven in base 10 but they have
been put into different number bases. *Can you
work out which base has been used for each pair?*

How to add in base two

```
  4 2 1
  1 0 1
+ 1 1 1
```

```
  8 4 2 1
    1 0 1
+   1 1 1
  1 1 0 0
```

When you get 2 ones in a column you add a one to the next column. When you get 2 ones in the highest value column you make a new column. *Can you do the following additions?*

$$1100 + 10001$$

$$100101 + 101100$$

$$10000 + 10110$$

$$110000 + 1010110$$

How to subtract in base two

```
  4 2 1
  1 1 0
- 1 0 1
```

```
  8 4 2 1
    1 1 0
-   1 0 1
        1
```
You take 1 from the 2's column

Can you do the following subtractions?

$$111 - 11$$

$$101110 - 100010$$

$$11101 - 1011$$

$$10010 - 1001$$

Puzzling?

New job
At noon John tells four friends that he has got a new job. By 12.05 pm the four friends have each given the information to a further four people. So 20 people now know that John has a new job. By 12.10 pm all 20 people have each told another four people.

If the information is passed on in this way every five minutes, how many people will know that John has got a new job by 1.00 pm?

Doubling
A very special water lily doubles its size every day. After 30 days it will completely cover a circular lake. *How much of the lake would it cover after 15 days?*

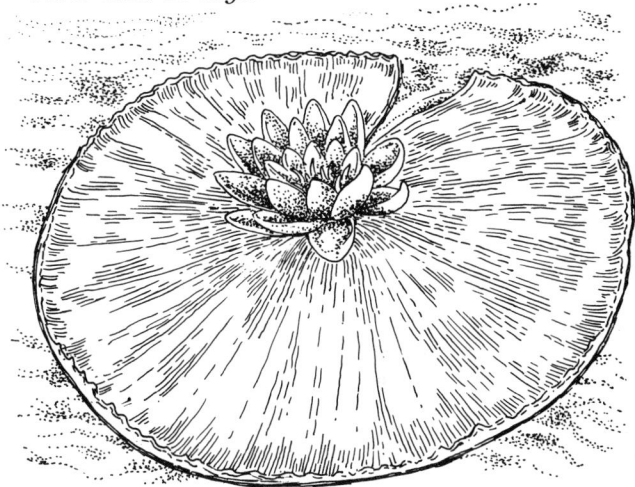

Millions more
Assuming that there is a new set of parents every 25 years, this family tree proves that there were millions more people alive a thousand years ago than there are now. *Or does it?*

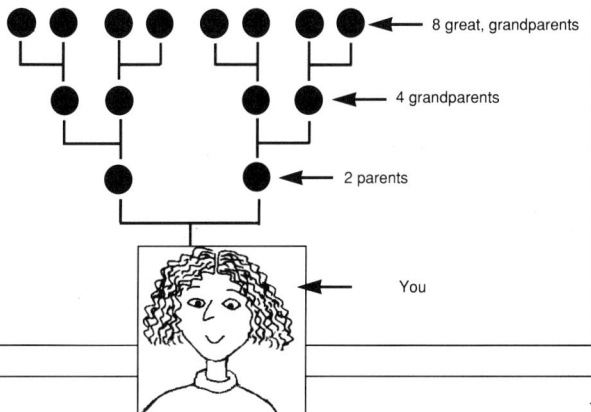

← 8 great, grandparents

← 4 grandparents

← 2 parents

You

Number patterns

In this number pattern the starting place is 10. The generating rule is 'add 10 to the previous number'.

All mathematical patterns have a starting place and a generating rule. It is possible to create patterns by choosing your own starting place and generating rule. Whether patterns have been created by you or somebody else it is interesting to explore the pattern further. When you have looked at the pattern closely you may find that by making observations about how the pattern grows it is possible to predict any number in the sequence. The pattern in the windows is:

1   10
2   20
3   ?

How would you work out what was in a particular window if they carried on forever?

Patterns can be made with shapes instead of numbers. Here are some more pattern windows for you to think about ...

Make up some mathematical patterns of your own. See if you can predict any number in your sequences. See if a friend can work them out.

Digital roots

If we look at sets of numbers according to a rule we may also observe patterns that we didn't realise were there.

All numbers have digital roots. This is how you can find the digital root of a number:

Add the digits until a single digit number is reached.

48	4 + 8	
12	1 + 2	
3		

3 is the digital root of 48.

You can find the digital root of sequences of numbers and see some interesting patterns emerge.

3 times table

3 (0+3)	6 (0+6)	9 (0+9)	12 (1+2)	15 (1+5)	18 (1+8)	21 (2+1)	24 (2+4)
3	6	9	3	6	9	3	6

How will the pattern of digital roots of the 3 times table continue?

4 times table

4 (0+4)	8 (0+8)	12 (1+2)	16 (1+6)	20 (2+0)	24 (2+4)	28 (2+8)	32 (3+2)
4	8	3	7	2	6	10 (1+0) → 1	5

Investigate other times tables.

Triangle numbers

1 / ?	3 / ?	6 / ?	10 / ?	15 / ?	21 / ?	28 / ?	36 / ?

... Square ...

What happens with other types of numbers?

Exploring rules ...

Can you see how these rules were generated?

2	3	5	8	3	1	4	5	9	4	3	7	0	7	7	4

8	2	0	2	2	4	6	0	6	6	2	8	0	8	8	6

When you have discovered the rule use the same rule to see what would happen for different pairs of starting numbers.

These patterns were created in a similar way. *Can you discover the rule?*

2	3	0	3	3	1	4	0	4	4	3	2	0	2	2	4

1	4	5	2	0	2	2	4	6	3	2	5	0	5	5	3

... and building upwards

When you have created a pattern according to a rule you can use the pattern to create a new pattern. The patterns below have been built in this way.

What will happen to each triangle as it grows?

What will happen if you make more triangles?

1	= 1
1 1	= 2
1 1 1	= 3
1 1 1 1	= 4
1 1 1 1 1	= 5
1 1 1 1 1 1	= 6

1	= 1
2 1	= 3
3 2 1	= 6
4 3 2 1	= 10
5 4 3 2 1	= 15
6 5 4 3 2 1	= 21

1	= 1
3 1	= 4
6 3 1	= 10
10 6 3 1	= 20
15 10 6 3 1	= 35
21 15 10 6 3 1	= 56

On average

The word 'average' comes from an Arabic word meaning damaged goods, which was used by traders in medieval Venice. It was one of the earliest forms of insurance. Groups of merchants who were sending goods by sea would agree that if any particular merchant's goods were damaged or washed overboard the other merchants would club together and thus spread the cost of replacing the lost or damaged goods.

Recent statistics published by an international aid organisation give the average birth rate per woman in the United Kingdom as 1.9 children. *Have you ever come across 0.9 of a child?*

The answer to the question above is obviously 'no'. How was this average arrived at and how is it useful? There are three types of average with each having its own uses. The types are *mean*, *mode* and *median*.

Mean
The mean is found by collecting a set of data, such as the heights of students in a class, adding that data together and then dividing by the number of items, in this example the number of students.

Mode
The mode is found by looking at a set of data and finding which occurs most often.

Median
The median is found by putting a set of data in order of size and finding the middle item. If you have an even number of data and there are two items in the middle, the median is midway between these two.

On average how long does it take a person to eat a scoop of ice cream?

What is the average number of people sitting at a table?

THE DOOPA DOUBLE SCOOP
- blackberry
- chocolate
- fudge
- raspberry
- strawberry
- pistachio
- vanilla

What is the average number of chairs at a table?

Class 7R
There are fifteen students in class 7R. Each was measured by the teacher using a metric rule. *Can you find the mean height, the mode height and the median height of the class? Which five pupils are of average height?*

Bob 1.9m Susie 1.5m Emily 1.8m Megan 1.7m Alexia 1.4m Lilah 1.4m Liling 1.5m Charlie 1.9m Carmel 1.4m Dimitri 1.8m Jose 2m Ahmed 1.6m Kim 1.4m Mamooda 1.3m Maria 1.7m

THE AVERAGE ICE CREAM PARLOUR

What is the average wait for a banana split if it can take 5 minutes, 7 minutes or 11 minutes – depending on how busy the palour is?

Try a PEACH MELBA or a BANANA SPLIT

Which ice cream is favourite with the customers?

ORDERS

Table 1
DOUBLE SCOOP OF RASP. AND CHOC. TRIPLE SCOOP OF STRAW, CHOC AND VANILLA

Table 2
SINGLE SCOOP OF CHOC. DOUBLE SCOOP OF RASP. AND B.BERRY. DOUBLE SCOOP OF FUDGE AND CHOC

Table 3
DOUBLE SCOOP OF PIST. AND STRAW. TRIPLE SCOOP OF STRAW, CHOC AND FUDGE

BAR
BANANA SPLIT WITH TWO SCOOPS OF VANILLA

Pay rise

This is a list of the 10 staff and their hourly pay rates at the ice-cream parlour.

Number	Job	Hourly pay
1	Manager	£10
4	Waiter	£5
3	Cook	£3
2	Washer	£2

The owner had agreed that everyone of the staff could have a pay rise of 10% of the average hourly pay.

During a quiet period the cooks each worked out what they thought the hourly rise would be.

IT'LL BE 40p

NO, IT WILL BE 43p

NONSENSE – IT SHOULD BE 50p

Which type of average had each of the cooks used to calculate the rise?

Which average do you think would be fairest? How much would the owner pay?

How much would the owner pay if he just raised each of the hourly rates by 10% instead of finding an average?

39

The Maya

Until the arrival of Christopher Columbus in 1492 the peoples of North and South America had not been influenced by any outside cultures. Different civilisations in the Americas came and went. These included those of the Olmec, Maya, Toltec, Mixtec and Aztec.

Of these civilisations the Maya were the most advanced in mathematics. At its peak, between AD 300 to 1000, the civilisation covered an area in South America as large as the United Kingdom.

The Maya did not have any metal tools or weapons. Nor did they have wheels. The Maya were completely dependent on human labour for their agricultural output and transportation. Yet they were able to build cities bigger than many in Europe at the same time. The Maya also developed a written language which they used to record events in their calendar. The Mayan calendar system was far more accurate than the Julian calendar used by the invaders from Western Europe in the 16th century.

Our knowledge of the Mayan world is not very full. The Spanish, who first arrived, did not try to understand the existing culture and they destroyed nearly all of the written records. Only three manuscripts survive. Most of our information comes from either Spanish accounts of previous accounts passed on by word of mouth, or from the study of Mayan hieroglyphics carved onto stone.

These hieroglyphics were very difficult to decipher, but fortunately a spoken version descended from the Mayan language survived. Using this we now know the meanings of 500 of the 800 known hieroglyphics.

As with many civilisations, written records, and especially carved ones, were made at the direction of the various priesthoods and were to do with their calendar, recording great events or when official religious events should take place during the year. Because of this we may have a distorted view of a people totally dominated by the calculation of the year.

Mayan number system

The Maya developed a written system of numbers based on 18 and 20.

In our decimal system place values go up in tens and 61 924 would be written under the following place headings:

10 000	1000	100	10	1
6	1	9	2	4

In the Mayan system these are the first five place values with the number 61 924 under the headings:

18×20^3 $= 144\,000$	18×20^2 $= 7200$	18×20 $= 360$	20	1
0	8	12	0	4

The Maya did not write their numbers with the Hindu-Arabic numerals that we use. Their system was much simpler.

● (a dot or pebble) stood for one and | (a stick) stood for five. ◉ (a shell) stood for zero and was used as a place

holder when there were no numbers of that value. The Maya wrote their numbers from bottom to top. This is how they would have written the number 61 924:

••• (dots over bar)	$8 \times 7200 = 57\ 600$
•• (two dots over bar)	$12 \times 360 = 4320$
(shell symbol)	$0 \times 20 = 0$
•••• (four dots)	$4 \times 1 = 4$

Can you translate these Mayan numbers into our decimal system?

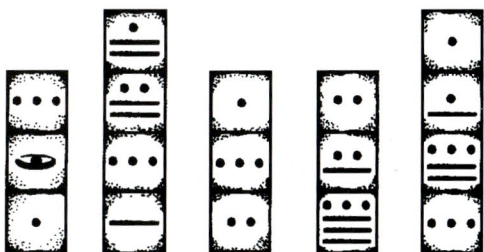

Surprising numbers

$$1^2 = 1$$
$$11^2 = 121$$
$$111^2 = 12321$$
$$1111^2 = 1234321$$
$$11111^2 = 123454321$$
$$111111^2 = 12345654321$$

$$9^3 = 729$$
$$99^3 = 970299$$
$$999^3 = 997002999$$
$$9999^3 = 999700029999$$

$$4^2 = 16$$
$$34^2 = 1156$$
$$334^2 = 111556$$
$$3334^2 = 11115556$$
$$33334^2 = 1111155556$$

$$9^2 = 81$$
$$99^2 = 9801$$
$$999^2 = 998001$$
$$9999^2 = 99980001$$
$$99999^2 = 9999800001$$

$$3 \times 37 = 111$$
$$6 \times 37 = 222$$
$$9 \times 37 = 333$$
$$12 \times 37 = 444$$
$$15 \times 37 = 555$$
$$18 \times 37 = 666$$

$$1 \div 9 = 0.11111\ \dots$$
$$2 \div 9 = 0.22222\ \dots$$
$$3 \div 9 = 0.33333\ \dots$$
$$4 \div 9 = 0.44444\ \dots$$
$$5 \div 9 = 0.55555\ \dots$$

$$1 + 2 = 3$$
$$4 + 5 + 6 = 7 + 8$$
$$9 + 10 + 11 + 12 = 13 + 14 + 15$$
$$16 + 17 + 18 + 19 + 20 = 21 + 22 + 23 + 24$$

Do all these patterns continue?

$$483 \times 12 = 5796$$
$$297 \times 18 = 5346$$
$$157 \times 28 = 4396$$

What do you notice about these multiplications? Can you make any more?

```
  12345679
×        8
  98765432
×        9
 888888888
```

```
 123456789
 123456789
 987654321
 987654321
+        2
2222222222
```

Do these add up?

$$3 \times 1 = 3$$
$$3 \times 2 = 6$$
$$3 \times 3 = 9$$
$$3 \times 4 = 12$$
$$3 \times 5 = 15$$
$$3 \times 6 = 18$$

$$1 + 2 = 3$$
$$1 + 5 = 6$$
$$1 + 8 = 9$$

$$3 \times 99 = 297 \qquad 2 + 9 + 7 = 18 \qquad 1 + 8 = 9$$
$$3 \times 100 = 300\ \dots$$

Have you spotted the pattern?

41

Problems with primes

What do the numbers 41 and 112 303 have in common? Both are prime numbers. These numbers have fascinated mathematicians ever since their discovery by the Ancient Greeks. The first 20 are shown in this table, which is called a sieve.

1	2	3	4	5	6
7	8	9	10	11	12
13	14	15	16	17	18
19	20	21	22	23	24
25	26	27	28	29	30
31	32	33	34	35	36
37	38	39	40	41	42
43	44	45	46	47	48
49	50	51	52	53	54
55	56	57	58	59	60
61	62	63	64	65	66
67	68	69	70	71	72

What is a prime number?

A prime number is a number which has exactly two different factors, itself and one. So no other whole number can be divided into it without leaving a remainder. One of the most fascinating things about prime numbers is that they do not appear to form any regular pattern in their occurrence. There is also no easy test which can be used to find out whether a given number is prime or not. It is therefore extremely difficult to find out whether some large numbers are prime.

> 11 is a prime number ...
> 101 is a prime number ...
>
> ... Are 1001 or 10001 prime numbers?

Eratosthenes was a Greek scholar who lived from 276 BC to 194 BC, and was a friend of Archimedes. He pioneered scientific geography and became Head of the Library of Alexandria.

Eratosthenes made a close study of prime numbers, and devised a 'sieve' to find them. Using a table of numbers, his method works as follows:

- Cross out all the multiples of 2 except for the number 2.
- Cross out all the multiples of 3 except for the number 3.
- You will find that all the multiples of 4 are already crossed out.
- Cross out all the multiples of 5 except for the number 5. Carry on this method for all the numbers up to the value of the square root of the highest number in the table.
- All the numbers not crossed out are prime.

While there is no predictable pattern for primes there are some interesting patterns which hold for a short time. By copying out a number table and colouring in the prime numbers on different-sized grids it is possible to see these patterns.

> **The highest prime number so far found (in 1992) is $2^{756839} - 1$. It contains 227 832 digits.**

Euclid, who lived about 330 BC to 275 BC was a teacher of mathematics in the Museum, in Alexandria. His main contribution to mathematics was to collect all the important work already done by Greek mathematicians into a series of books called the *Elements*.

In the *Elements*, book nine, Euclid covered the theory of number. He wrote a clear and undisputed proof that showed that there is an infinite number of prime numbers.

The proof was by contradiction. Say you thought that that you had the biggest prime number – we'll

The first modern university was founded in Alexandria in 300 BC. It was called the Museum after the Greek goddesses of Arts and Science, the Muses.

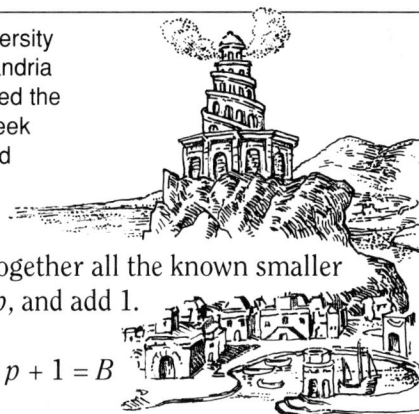

call it p. Multiply together all the known smaller primes, including p, and add 1.

$$2 \times 3 \times 5 \times 7 \times ... \times p + 1 = B$$

B cannot be divided by any of the smaller primes so it must therefore be a bigger prime. Thus p cannot be the biggest prime.

There are also some other questions you could explore. All numbers can be made by multiplying prime numbers together ... 24 can be made by $2 \times 2 \times 2 \times 3$. It has 4 prime factors. *Which numbers below 100 have the largest number of prime factors?*

Two thousand years after Euclid prime numbers still intrigued mathematicians. Before computers, testing a six- or seven-digit number took weeks of calculation, and many numbers that were thought of as prime were later proved not to be so.

Goldbach, an 18th century mathematician, suggested that every even number can be made by adding two prime numbers together.

    2 is 1 + 1
    4 is 2 + 2
    6 is 3 + 3
    8 is 3 + 5

Can you make all of the even numbers up to 100 like this? (A list of prime numbers up to 100 would help.)

You will have noticed that Goldbach used 1 as a prime number. There are arguments about whether 1 can be thought of as prime or not. *What do you think?*

In the 19th century it was suggested that every even number can be made by subtracting two consecutive prime numbers in an infinite number of ways. For example, 6 can be made by subtracting 11 from 17 or 13 from 19.

Just using the prime numbers from 1 to 100, can you find out how many different ways there are of making the number 6 by subtracting two consecutive prime

numbers? It is also possible to make other even numbers, and if you have a larger list of prime numbers you can explore how many different ways you can find for making each even number in this way.

It has also been stated that half of the prime numbers can be made up by adding two square numbers together. For example you can make 5 with $1^2 + 2^2$ and 17 with $1^2 + 4^2$. *Do you think this is true?*

Dudeney puzzles

Henry Ernest Dudeney, a mathematician and author of many mathematical puzzle books, posed the following interesting problem about digits and primes.

You must use each of the 9 digits once and once only. Make a set of prime numbers which will add to the smallest possible total. For example:

$$
\begin{array}{r}
61 \\
283 \\
47 \\
+ 59 \\
\hline
450
\end{array}
$$

Is it possible to make a smaller total than this?

Dudeney was also credited with having constructed a 3×3 magic square using the following prime numbers:

1, 7, 13, 31, 37, 43, 61, 67 and 73

If all the horizontal, vertical and diagonal lines have to add up to the same number (the magic constant) what would Dudeney's magic square have been?

The path to infinity

In school the students are having an infinitely long day. They are finding it difficult to come to terms with the idea that the Universe goes on forever outwards as well as inwards. At the same time they are trying to grasp that they can never find either the largest or the smallest number. One student thinks he has found the biggest number, another adds one. If a student finds the smallest number then someone else divides it by ten.

Suppose there are an infinite number of students in school today. The first lesson is geography and every student is given a geography exercise book. It is then decided that all of the pupils will now study mathematics and art as well, so two further exercise books are given to each pupil. *How many books will be needed now?*

The infinite number of pupils in Infinity School have numbers on their backs. The teacher asks the infinite number of pupils to join hands with the person who has one more than their number on their back. The teacher then changes the rule and asks all of the pupils to join hands with the person who has the number which is three more than them on their back. *How many pupils end up playing in the second game?*

Each mirror image is half the size of the previous one. *If all the mirror images were stacked on top of each other how tall would they be in relation to the full size figure?*

In the mathematics classroom the pupils are looking for the smallest number. *Will they ever find it?*

0.5

0.05

0.005

0.0005

0.00005

005

A few solutions

Page 4 *Names for numbers* Finger 1, Eyes 2, Feyes 3, Limbs 4, Flimbs 5, Elimbs 6, Feyelimbs 7, Limblimbs 8, Flimblimbs 9, Flimbflimbs 10

Page 5 *Pounds, shillings and pence*
£14/5/6d (Fourteen pounds, five shillings and six pence)
£10/18/3d (Ten pounds, eighteen shillings and three pence)
£29/19/3d (Twenty nine pounds, nineteen shillings and three pence)
£3/9/6d (Three pounds, nine shillings and six pence)

Page 6 *Zero sums*

$100 + 0 = 100$	$100 \div 0 = \infty$	$0 \times 100 = 0$
$0 - 100 = -100$	$0 + 100 = 100$	$0 \div 100 = 0$
$100 \times 0 = 0$	$100 - 0 = 100$	

Page 7 *On the cards* The following are all the 2-digit numbers in the Fibonacci series: 13, 21, 34, 55, 89. The number 13 is prime because it has exactly two distinct factors: 1 and 13.

13×13 is 169 which is a 3-digit number

(89 is also prime, but its square is a 4-digit number, 7921)

Page 8 *Consecutive numbers for m and n*
when $m = 2$ and $n = 1$ $\quad m^2 - n^2 = 3 \quad 2mn = 4 \quad m^2 + n^2 = 5$
when $m = 3$ and $n = 2$ $\quad m^2 - n^2 = 5 \quad 2mn = 12 \quad m^2 + n^2 = 13$
when $m = 4$ and $n = 3$ $\quad m^2 - n^2 = 7 \quad 2mn = 24 \quad m^2 + n^2 = 25$
when $m = 5$ and $n = 4$ $\quad m^2 - n^2 = 9 \quad 2mn = 40 \quad m^2 + n^2 = 41$

Triangle numbers for m and n
Here are the first few triangle numbers: 1, 3, 6, 10, 15, 21 and 28

when $m = 3$ and $n = 1$ $\quad m^2 - n^2 = 8 = 2 \times 4 \qquad 2mn = 6 = 2 \times 3$
$\qquad\qquad\qquad\qquad m^2 + n^2 = 10 = 2 \times 5$
when $m = 6$ and $n = 3$ $\quad m^2 - n^2 = 27 = 3 \times 9 \qquad 2mn = 36 = 3 \times 12$
$\qquad\qquad\qquad\qquad m^2 + n^2 = 45 = 3 \times 15$
when $m = 10$ and $n = 6$ $\quad m^2 - n^2 = 64 = 4 \times 16 \qquad 2mn = 120 = 4 \times 30$
$\qquad\qquad\qquad\qquad m^2 + n^2 = 136 = 4 \times 34$

Page 9
Square to square   *Perigal's dissection*   *Triangles to spirals*

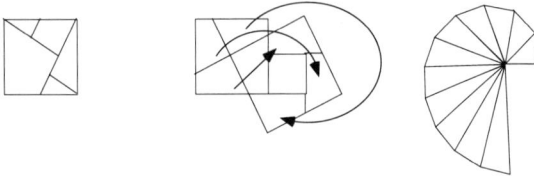

Page 10 *Perfect numbers* 496 and 8 128

Imperfect numbers Deficient: 35 (sum of factors 13), 42 (sum of factors 41), 64 (sum of factors 63), 99 (sum of factors 57), 155 (sum of factors 37)
Abundant: 56 (sum of factors 64), 70 (sum of factors 74), 84 (sum of factors 140), 102 (sum of factors 114), 112 (sum of factors 136)

Page 11 *Attica symbols* Top left: 22 284, top right: 3142, bottom left: 17 296, bottom right: 18 416

Ancient Greek puzzle 120 olives

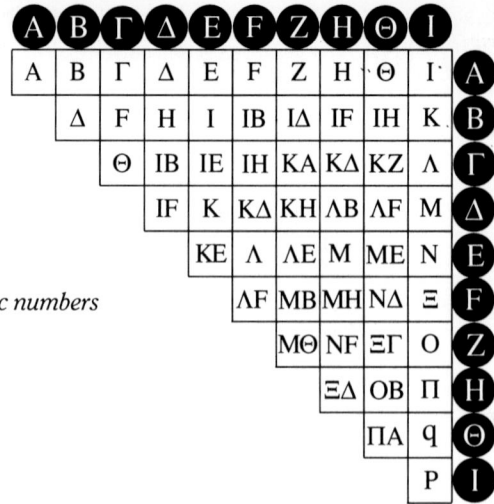

Ionic numbers

×	A	B	Γ	Δ	E	F	Z	H	Θ	I
A	A	B	Γ	Δ	E	F	Z	H	Θ	I
B		Δ	F	H	I	IB	IΔ	IF	IH	K
Γ			Θ	IB	IE	IH	KA	KΔ	KZ	Λ
Δ				IF	K	KΔ	KH	ΛB	ΛF	M
E					KE	Λ	ΛE	M	ME	N
F						ΛF	MB	MH	NΔ	Ξ
Z							MΘ	NF	ΞΓ	O
H								ΞΔ	OB	Π
Θ									ΠΑ	ϙ
I										Ρ

Page 12 *How many grains?* 25 000 000 000 000 (If 20 grains of sand equals a grain of wheat and 125 grains of wheat makes a cubic centimetre.)

Page 13 *Sky high numbers* Mercury: 5.8×10^7, Venus: 1.1×10^8, Jupiter: 7.7×10^8, Saturn: 1.4×10^9, Uranus: 2.8×10^9, Neptune: 4.4×10^9, Pluto: 5.9×10^9, Altair: 1.5×10^{14}, Sirius: 8.2×10^{13}, Procyon: 1.04×10^{14}, Beta Centauri: 3.7×10^{15}

Page 14 *Abacus* Chinese: 123456789, Russian: 7483621954, Japanese: 7946.8723457694

Page 15 *A number puzzle* Here are three ways:

3 4 1	3 1 8	2 7 3
5 8 6	6 5 4	5 4 6
9 2 7	9 7 2	8 1 9

Page 16 *Smith's prize* It would depend on how long you expected to live. (A) would be worth £15 300 in year 4 and £30 500 in year 5, (B) would be worth £15 625 in year 4 and £39 062.50 in year 5, (C) would be worth £800 in year 4 and £1600 in year 5.
After five years prize (B) would be the best, but if you lived longer would it still be?

A working year Though Clare made it seem all very reasonable she in fact counted the same hours several times. Having calculated 8 hours a day for sleeping and 8 hours a day for leisure she discounted two thirds of the year – equivalent to 244 days. Some of these days will be Saturdays and Sundays and so Clare should not have deducted another 52 Saturdays and Sundays.

By counting the same hours for holidays, leisure and eating you can see how easy it was for Clare to reduce Tom's working year to zero.

Page 17 *Profit or loss* Stamp A: £6000 = 120% of original price paid by Kate, Stamp B: £6000 = 80% of original price paid by Kate. Stamp A originally cost £5000; stamp B originally cost £7500. Kate made an overall loss of £500.

One is light 3 weighings, here is how:

Lightest 8   Lightest 2 or 3

Missing dime The original bill should be ignored when working out the total paid. With the discount the actual bill was $8.50; plus the 20 cent unofficial tip.

Page 18 *Cryptarithms* BAG × GAB B = 2, A = 3, G = 4
4539281706 × 2 (Are there any other answers?)
SEND + MORE = MONEY S = 9, E = 5, N = 6, D = 7
TEN + TEN + FORTY = SIXTY T = 8, E = 5, N = 0
WRONG + WRONG = RIGHT One solution is W = 2, R = 5, O = 9N = 3, G = 8
SEAM × T = MEATS S = 4, E = 9, A = 7, M = 3, T = 8
GREEN × RED = ORANGE G = 4, R = 7, E = 0, N = 5
ABC × DE A = 1, B = 2, C = 5, D = 3, E = 7

Page 25 *Spy lights* 471

Page 27 *Added to 3* $x = 4$, *Four times* $x = 4$, *Seven times* $x = 5$ *How old?* Mother is 36 years, elder daughter is 12 and younger daughter is 2. *Mother and son* Mother is 50 years and son is 30 years. *Red and green* 36 red, 12 green. *Differ by one* 8:10. *20 more* 9×20

Page 28 *Pyramids* 1 crystal would make a square based pyramid and 4900 would also make a square based pyramid. 1 crystal would make a triangle based pyramid and 4 would also make a triangle based pyramid.

Cube statues There are 27 cubes in a size 3 cube. There are 1000 cubes in a size 10 cube. If the shape was hollow a size 3 cube would contain 26 small cubes and a size 10 cube would contain 488.

Page 29 *Flags* $\frac{1}{3}, \frac{2}{3}, \dots$ *Turrets* Square numbers *Windows* $\frac{2}{5}, \frac{3}{5}, \dots$ *Path* Fibonacci numbers *Garden* Figurative numbers

Page 31 *Some puzzling circle*

Floating island   A magic circle

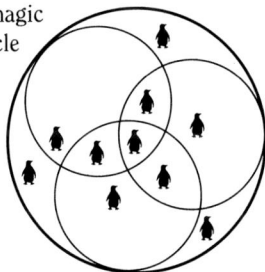

Page 32 *The Mathematician's Tale* $10! = 3\,628\,800$
Eating out 7 August
Alphabet $26! = 4.032914611 \times 10^{26}$

Arranging fences

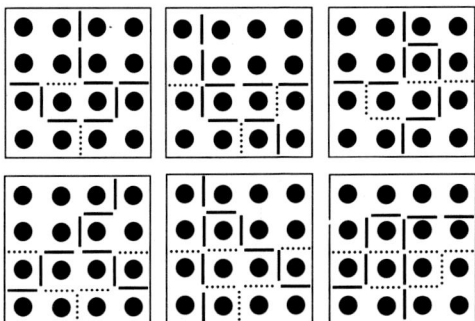

Page 34 *Dice number base* First: base 4, Second: base 2, Third: base 3, Fourth: base 5

Page 35 *Base two additions* 11101, 1010001, 100110, 10000110
Base two subtractions 100, 1100, 10010, 1001

New job
12.05	16 + 4	= 20
12.10	80 + 20	= 100
12.15	400 + 100	= 500
⋮		
1.00		= 976 562 500

Doubling $\dfrac{1}{32\,768}$

Page 36 *Pattern windows* Building on left: 1, 3, 5 ..., 3, 6, 9 ..., 1, 2, 4, 7, 11 ...,Building in centre: Half, third quarter, ..., Fibonacci numbers, three sides, four sides, five sides ... Building on right: If even halve if odd multiply by 5 and add 1, prime numbers.

Page 37 *Exploring rules* The first two patterns are made using the following rule: add the two previous digits and put down the units digit as the next number. The next two patterns are: add the two previous digits in base 5 and put down the units digit of the answer as the next number; add the two previous digits in base 7 and put down the units digit of the answer as the next number.

Building upwards For each triangle there is a way of working out what each row will add to and then it will be possible to find a pattern for each triangle.

$$\begin{aligned} 1 &= 1 \\ 11 &= 2 \\ 111 &= 3 \end{aligned}$$

Page 38 *Class 7R* Mean: 1.62, Mode: 1.4, Median: 1.6
Alexia, Carmel, Kim, Lilah (Mode), Ahmed (Median)

The average ice-cream parlour Eating a single scoop: It is difficult to answer this question as no data is given. You could buy an ice cream and time yourself eating it. You could get some friends to do the same. *Would you have a good average? Do younger people eat ice cream faster than older people? Just how big is a scoop of ice cream?*

Pay rise Median: 40p, Mean: 43p, Mode: 50p

Page 41 *Mayan numbers* (From left to right) 1081, 83585, 422, 878, 9723

Page 42 *What is a prime number?* 1001 is not a prime number because $143 \times 7 = 1001$. 10001 is not a prime number because $73 \times 137 = 10001$

Page 43 *Most prime factors* $2 \times 2 \times 2 \times 2 \times 2 \times 2 = 64$
$2 \times 2 \times 2 \times 2 \times 2 \times 3 = 96$

Making six There are 11 different ways: 89 − 83, 79 − 73, 67 − 61, 59 − 53, 53 − 47, 37 − 31, 29 − 23, 23 − 17, 19 − 13, 17 − 11 and 11 − 5

Dudeney puzzles 2 + 47 + 59 + 61 + 83, 111

Page 45 *Mirror images* Height of all mirror images on top of each other would be equal to the height of the full size figure.

A page of numbers

Arabic (Gobar)	Arabic (Modern)	Babylonian	Chinese (Rod)	Chinese	Egyptian (Hierogl-yphics)	Egyptian (Hieratic)	Greek (Attic)	Greek (Ionian)	Hebrew	Hindu (Gwalior)	Inter-national (modern)	Mayan	Roman
1	١	▼	l	一	l	l	l	A	א	۱	1	•	I
2	٢	▼▼	ll	二	ll	Ꙋ	ll	B	ב	٢	2	••	II
3	٣	▼▼▼	lll	三	lll	lll	lll	Γ	ג	٣	3	•••	III
4	٤	▼▼▼▼	llll	四	llll	llll	llll	Δ	ד	٨	4	••••	IV
5	٥	▼▼▼▼▼	lllll	五	lll ll	ly	Γ	E	ה	٩	5	—	V
6	٦	▼▼▼	⊤	六	lll lll	ny	Γl	F	ו	٤	6	⋅—	VI
7	٧	▼▼▼▼	⊤⊤	七	llll lll	2	Γll	Z	ז	⋺	7	••—	VII
8	٨	▼▼▼▼	⊤⊤⊤	八	llll llll	≡	Γlll	H	ח	⋷	8	•••—	VIII
9	٩	▼▼▼▼▼	⊤⊤⊤⊤	九	llll lllll	⋌⋌	Γllll	Θ	ט	ᴅ	9	••••—	IX
10	١٠	◄	—	十	∩	ᴧ	Δ	I	י	٦٠	10	═	X
20	٢٠	◄◄	=	二十	∩∩	ᴧ̀	ΔΔ	K	כ	٢٠	20	⊙	XX
30	٣٠	◄◄◄	≡	三十	∩∩∩	ᴧ̣	ΔΔΔ	Λ	ל	٣٠	30	≐	XXX
40	٤٠	◄◄◄◄	≣	四十	∩∩∩∩	⊥	ΔΔΔΔ	M	מ	٨٠	40	⊙	XL
50	٥٠	◄◄◄◄	≣	五十	∩∩∩ ∩∩	㇅	Γᴧ	N	נ	٤٠	50	⋰	L
60	٦٠	▼	⊥	六十	∩∩∩ ∩∩∩	⊥⊥	Γᴧ Δ	Ξ	ס	٤٠	60	⊙	LX
70	٧٠	▼◄	⊥	七十	∩∩∩∩ ∩∩∩	ʒ	Γᴧ ΔΔ	O	ע	٢٠	70	•••	LXX
80	٨٠	▼◄◄	⊥	八十	∩∩∩∩ ∩∩∩∩	ᴤᴤ	Γᴧ ΔΔΔ	Π	פ	٤٠	80	••••	LXXX
90	٩٠	▼◄◄◄	≣	九十	∩∩∩∩∩ ∩∩∩∩∩	㇅	Γᴧ ΔΔΔΔ	ϟ	צ	٩٠٠	90	≣	XC
100	١٠٠	▼◄	l	百	9	⁄	H	P	ק	٦٠٠	100	⊙	C
200	٢٠٠	▼▼▼◄	ll	二百	99	⁄⁄	HH	Σ	ר	٢٠٠	200	⊙	CC
300	٣٠٠	▼▼▼	lll	三百	999	ᴤ	HHH	T	ש	٣٠٠	300	═	CCC
400	٤٠٠	▼▼▼◄◄	llll	四百	9999	ᴤ	HHHH	Y	ת	٨٠٠	400	⋰	CD
500	٥٠٠	▼▼▼▼◄◄	lllll	五百	999 99	ᴥ	⌐ᴴ	Φ	ך	٤٠٠	500	⊙	D
600	٦٠٠	◄	⊤	六百	999 999	ᴥ	⌐ᴴH	X	ם	٤٠٠	600	⊙	DC
700	٧٠٠	◄▼◄◄◄	⊤⊤	七百	9999 999	⌐Ʒ	⌐ᴴHH	Ψ	ן	٢٠٠	700	⋰	DCC
800	٨٠٠	◄▼▼▼◄◄	⊤⊤⊤	八百	9999 9999	ᴥ	⌐ᴴHHH	Ω	ף	٤٠٠	800	•••	DCCC
900	٩٠٠	◄▼▼▼▼	⊤⊤⊤⊤	九百	99999 99999	ᴥ	⌐ᴴHHHH	ᴧ	ץ	٩٠٠	900	⊙	CM

48